SECRETS OF
Italian
Meat and Poultry
Dishes

OVER 100 AUTHENTIC RECIPES

General Editor · Beverly LeBlanc

Macdonald Orbis

A Macdonald Orbis BOOK

Based upon *La Pentola d'Ora*, © Editoriale Del Drago, Milan 1983
English text and design © Macdonald & Co (Publishers) Ltd 1986, 1988

First published in Great Britain in 1988
by Macdonald & Co (Publishers) Ltd
London & Sydney

A member of BPCC plc

British Library Cataloguing in Publication Data

Secrets of Italian meat and poultry dishes.
(Secrets of series).
1. Cookery, Italian   2. Cookery (meat)
I. LeBlanc, Beverly
641.6'6'0945   TX 723

ISBN 0-356-15581-1

Illustrated by Alison Wisenfeld

Editor: Jennifer Jones
Designer: Clair Lidzey
Indexer: Myra Clark

Printed and bound in Great Britain by
Purnell Book Production Ltd, Paulton, Bristol
A member of BPCC plc

Macdonald & Co (Publishers) Ltd
Greater London House
Hampstead Road
London NW1 7QX

CONTENTS

Symbols

The symbols show how easy a recipe is, and the preparation and cooking times:

easy

more difficult

for experienced cooks

preparation time

cooking time

When using this book, remember the following points: (1) all quantities are for four people, unless otherwise stated; (2) use only one set of ingredients for the recipes, since American imperial and metric measurements are not exact equivalents and (3) in the text of recipes, American quantities and ingredients are listed first, with the British equivalents in square brackets.

INTRODUCTION

The idea that Italian food consists of only pasta and pizzas is far from the truth. Italy also has a strong tradition in cooking meats, poultry and game; indeed, veal is almost the national dish – and some Italian meat classics, such as Vitello Tonnato and Ossobuco, are already international favourites.

Italy consists of a number of well-defined and individual regions, each with its own cultural and culinary traditions. In fact, for over a thousand years after the decline of the Roman Empire, Italy as such did not exist and was simply a fragmented assortment of independent states. Even after over 120 years of unification, these regions have still retained their character, and for the cook they offer an extremely rich and varied cuisine. Apart from veal, top-quality beef, lamb and pork are produced in Italy's fertile valleys, giving rise to many fine and distinctive dishes. These can be as simple as a roast or quite elaborate, such as Bollito Misto (a mixture of beef, tongue, sausage and veal cooked in a cream sauce – a great regional favourite of Piedmont). For really economical dishes, the province of Lazio offers an excellent tradition of peasant dishes using offal, such as oxtails, sweetbreads, brains and tripe. Salamis and sausages, the speciality of the Emilio-Romagno region, are often combined with other meats in unusual and interesting ways.

Italian cheeses, another famous product, are used imaginatively not only with meat dishes, but also with poultry and game. Some of the most famous dishes in Italy are made with chicken, and the many Italian ways of cooking game also offers a range of delicious dishes. In Tuscany, for example, quail and snipe are commonly roasted in oil and then eaten accompanied by fried bread and the cooking juices. Quail – and pigeon too – may also be cooked long and slow in salmi or in a wine sauce, making them into meals of some richness.

To do full justice to the range and scope of Italian cuisine, try these recipes yourself, the very best in Italian meat, poultry and game cooking – and good eating!

BUYING AND COOKING VEAL

American cuts to choose	Cooking methods
leg, loin, rib (rack), boneless shoulder	roast
steaks or cutlets (scalloppine), chops, cubes for kebabs	broil, fry
breast, riblets, chops, steaks or cutlets, shank	braise
veal for stew	stew

British cuts to choose	Cooking methods
best end, breast, leg (including topside or cushion), loin, shoulder or oyster, fillet	roast
chump chops, best end neck cutlets, loin chops, escalopes, fillet steak, cubes for kebabs	grill, fry
breast, riblets, knuckle, middle neck cutlets	braise
shin, pie veal, scrag	stew

Scaloppe alla Carlo Porta

Veal Scallopine Cooked in Foil with Spinach

00:25   00:30

American	Ingredients	Metric/Imperial
8	Veal scallopine (escalopes)	8
8	Slices of fontina cheese	8
8	Slices of parma ham	8
¼ tsp	Chopped sage	¼ tsp
1	Shallot or small onion	1
¼ cup	Butter	50 g / 2 oz
Scant 2 cups	Cooked spinach	400 g / 14 oz
1 cup	Fresh cream	225 ml / 8 fl oz
¼ cup	Grated parmesan cheese	25 g / 1 oz

1. Preheat the oven to 350°F / 180°C / Gas Mark 4.
2. Pound the scallopine flat and cover each one with a slice of fontina cheese and one of parma ham; add a small pinch of sage and roll up, securing with a toothpick.
3. Chop the shallot and fry in the butter, add the veal rolls and brown on a medium heat.
4. Put the spinach into another pan, add the cream and heat through gently. Sprinkle with parmesan cheese and stir well.
5. Spread the spinach mixture on a sheet of baking foil, lay the rolls of veal on top, close the foil and bake in the oven for 15 minutes.

Scaloppine al whisky

Veal Scallopine with Whisky

00:05   00:07

American	Ingredients	Metric/Imperial
	Flour	
1 lb	Veal scallopine (escalopes)	500 g / 1 lb
¼ cup	Butter	50 g / 2 oz
	Salt	
	Freshly ground pepper	
¼ cup	Whisky	50 ml / 2 fl oz

1. Flour the scallopine, pressing well to make the flour stick to the meat.
2. Melt the butter in a heavy-bottomed frying pan and allow to color slightly. When butter is foaming, slip in the scallopine and on a fairly high heat, fry on both sides for 5 minutes, season with salt and a twist of ground black pepper, add the whisky, cover and simmer for 5 minutes. Serve very hot with freshly cooked vegetables.

Spezzatino alla romana

Veal Stew Roman-Style

	00:10	02:00

American	Ingredients	Metric/Imperial
1	Onion	1
2	Cloves	2
¼ cup	Butter	50 g / 2 oz
1¾ lb	Veal (breast or shoulder) diced	800 g / 1¾ lb
½ tsp	Chopped rosemary	½ tsp
1 quart	Stock	1 litre / 1¾ pints
3	Eggs	3
1 tbsp	Wine vinegar	1 tbsp
1	Lemon	1
	Salt and pepper	
1 tbsp	Chopped parsley	1 tbsp

1. Slice the onion, stick cloves into one of the slices. Heat butter and, when very hot, sauté onion and cloves for 2-3 minutes, then add meat and brown, stirring all the time. Sprinkle with rosemary and pour over stock, cover and simmer for about 2 hours.
2. Meanwhile, put eggs, vinegar and lemon juice into a bowl, season with salt and pepper and beat well.
3. When meat is tender, pour over egg sauce and stir until the eggs begin to solidify. Serve on a hot serving dish sprinkled with chopped parsley.

Pancetta di vitello in gelatina

Jellied Breast of Veal

	00:45	02:10

American	Ingredients	Metric/Imperial
¼ lb	Cooked ham	100 g / 4 oz
¼ lb	Mortadella	100 g / 4 oz
3	Eggs	3
2 tbsp	Grated parmesan cheese	1½ tbsp
	Salt and pepper	
2 lb	Breast of veal	1 kg / 2 lb
3	Carrots	3
1	Onion	1
1	Celery stalk	1
1	Bunch of chopped parsley	1
5 tsp	Gelatin	5 tsp

1. Chop the ham and mortadella, put into a bowl with the eggs, parmesan, salt and pepper and mix well.
2. Wipe and trim excess fat from breast of veal, open out flat.
3. Stuff the breast of veal with the ham mixture, press down firmly and sew up with fine string, or secure with skewers.

4. Chop the carrots, onion, celery and parsley and put them in a large saucepan with plenty of water. Bring to the boil.
5. Wrap the breast of veal in a clean boiled cloth or muslin and secure firmly, lower into the boiling water and allow to cook for about 2 hours.
6. Remove from the pan, drain reserving 2½ cups [600 ml / 1 pint] stock. Unwrap the veal and put between 2 plates with a weight on top while it is cooling.
7. Dissolve the gelatin by sprinkling it on to 4-5 tablespoons boiling meat stock. Mix into the reserved stock and cool. Replace the vegetables.
8. Slice the veal and arrange on a deep serving dish, spoon gelatin and vegetables over the slices and refrigerate. Serve when meat and jelly have set. Some jelly can be chopped for decoration.

Punta di vitello arrosto

Roast Loin of Veal

Lombardy produces excellent veal and roast veal is a traditional dish of the district around Pavia.

00:10   01:30

American	Ingredients	Metric/Imperial
5 oz	Bacon	150 g / 5 oz
½ cup	Oil	125 ml / 4 fl oz
1	Onion	1
1	Garlic clove	1
3¼ lb	Loin of veal (boned and rolled)	1.5 kg / 3¼ lb
2 cups	Stock	450 ml / ¾ pint
½ cup	Dry white wine	125 ml / 4 fl oz
8	Thin slices of fat pork for larding	8
	Pepper to taste	

1. Preheat the oven to 400°F / 200°C / Gas Mark 6.
2. Chop the bacon into small pieces and fry in a casserole with heated oil and finely chopped onion. Add the crushed clove of garlic and continue to fry over gentle heat until the bacon begins to brown.
3. When the bacon has browned, turn up the heat and add the joint of veal, browning quickly on all sides. Add the stock (which can be made using stock cubes, if you wish) a little at a time, then the wine.
4. Lard the meat by placing 4 thin strips of fat pork over the joint.
5. Roast in the oven for 1 hour, turning the joint once and larding again with the remaining slices of fat pork to ensure a good color.
6. Sprinkle with pepper and add a little water if the meat shows signs of sticking to the pan.
7. Roast veal can be served either hot, garnished with strips of cooked mixed vegetables such as carrot, onion and green pepper, or cold with a variety of salads.

Vitello in peperonata

Veal with Peperonata

Peperonata is a delicious sauce made from sweet peppers.

| | 00:20 | | 01:30 | |

American	Ingredients	Metric/Imperial
1¾ lb	Shoulder veal	800 g / 1¾ lb
1 tbsp	Vegetable oil	1 tbsp
1 tbsp	Butter	1 tbsp
	Salt and pepper	
¼ cup	Dry red wine	50 ml / 2 fl oz
1 quart	Stock (cubes dissolved in hot water)	1 litre / 1¾ pints
4	Sweet yellow or red peppers	4
2	Tomatoes	2

1. Dice veal. Heat the oil and butter in a pan and sauté meat for 2-3 minutes. Season with salt and pepper, then add wine. Cover and cook for about 1 hour, adding stock from time to time.
2. Meanwhile, prepare peperonata. Chop peppers and remove seeds. Skin tomatoes and put with the peppers into a saucepan over a high heat, then lower and simmer for 20 minutes, adding hot water if required.
3. Season with salt and add to the meat. Simmer to reduce sauce to a good consistency, then serve hot.

Rostin negaa (arrostino annegato)

Veal Scallopine Drowned in Wine

A traditional Milanese dish.

| | 00:10 | | 00:20 | |

American	Ingredients	Metric/Imperial
1¼ lb	Tender sliced veal (leg)	600 g / 1¼ b
¼ lb	Cooked ham	100 g / 4 oz
½ cup	Butter	100 g / 4 oz
1 cup	Dry white wine and white vinegar, mixed half and half	225 ml / 8 fl oz
	Salt and pepper	

1. Pound the veal slices flat, cover each one with a slice of ham, roll and secure with fine kitchen string or toothpick.
2. Heat the butter in a frying pan and when it foams slip in the meat and brown over a high heat. Sprinkle with vinegar and wine, cover and simmer. Season with salt and pepper.

Rosemary, bay leaf and courgette

Spezzatino all'ortolana

Veal Stew with Vegetables

00:20   01:10

American	Ingredients	Metric/Imperial
1 ½ lb	Lean veal, diced	650 g / 1 ½ lb
	Salt and pepper	
	White flour	
¼ cup	Vegetable oil	50 ml / 2 fl oz
¼ cup	Butter	50 g / 2 oz
⅔ cup	Dry white wine	150 ml / ¼ pint
14 oz	Peeled plum tomatoes	400 g / 14 oz
1 quart	Stock	1 litre / 1 ¾ pints
1	Celery stalk	1
1	Carrot	1
1	Onion	1
2	Zucchini (courgettes)	2
½ tsp	Chopped rosemary	½ tsp
1	Bay leaf	1

1. Dip veal in seasoned flour. Heat half the oil and butter in a heavy-based pan and brown veal all over. Add wine and evaporate quickly over a high heat, then add chopped tomatoes and stock. Cover and leave to simmer.

2. Meanwhile, wash and chop vegetables. Heat remaining oil and butter in another pan, fry vegetables with rosemary, bay leaf and pepper. After 10 minutes, transfer vegetables with a slotted spoon to the pan containing the meat. Stir well and simmer for about 1 hour.

3. Transfer to a hot casserole dish and serve.

Frittata di vitello alla salvia

Veal Omelette with Sage

00:15   00:18

American	Ingredients	Metric/Imperial
1 lb	Roast veal	450 g / 1 lb
5	Eggs	5
1	Bunch of sage leaves	1
1 tbsp	Milk	1 tbsp
1 tsp	Flour	1 tsp
1 tbsp	Cognac	1 tbsp
	Salt and pepper	
1 cup	Vegetable oil	225 ml / 8 fl oz
2 – 3 tbsp	Béchamel sauce	1½ – 2 tbsp

1. Chop the roast meat very finely or grind (mince) or put through a food processor. Add the beaten egg yolks, the stiffly whipped whites, and a handful of whole sage leaves. Beat with milk and flour to obtain a smooth mixture. Mix in the cognac and season with salt and pepper to taste.
2. Put oil in a frying pan and when it is smoking pour in the mixture, lowering the flame and shaking the pan so that it does not stick. Turn as for an ordinary omelette or if preferred cook the top under the broiler (grill) under a high heat.
3. Preheat the oven to 350°F / 180°C / Gas Mark 4.
4. Transfer the omelette to an ovenproof serving dish lined with aluminium foil. Close the foil by folding and place in the oven for 12 minutes. Pour béchamel over the omelette.

Crocchette di vitello

Veal Croquettes

00:35   00:35

American	Ingredients	Metric/Imperial
½ lb	Raw ground (minced) ham	225 g / 8 oz
½ lb	Ground (minced) veal	225 g / 8 oz
2	Eggs	2
1	Lemon	1
½ cup	Soft bread crumbs	50 g / 2 oz
¼ cup	Grated parmesan cheese	25 g / 1 oz
½ tsp	Chopped basil	½ tsp
	Salt and pepper	
1 cup	Dried bread crumbs	100 g / 4 oz
1 cup	Vegetable oil	225 ml / 8 fl oz

1. Mix the ground ham and veal with the eggs, grated lemon rind, bread crumbs, parmesan, basil, salt and pepper, shape into croquettes and coat them in the dried bread crumbs.
2. Preheat the oven to 350°F / 180°C / Gas Mark 4.
3. Put the oil in a frying pan and fry the croquettes until golden brown.
4. Place on absorbent kitchen towels to drain. Arrange hot croquettes on a piece of foil, sprinkle with lemon juice, fold the foil to close and cook in the oven for 15 minutes. Serve immediately with rice and a green salad.

Vitello tonnato

Cold Veal in Tuna Sauce

00:20   02:00

American	Ingredients	Metric/Imperial
1 ½ lb	Veal joint, preferably top round	600 g / 1 ½ lb
1	Carrot	1
1	Onion	1
1	Celery stalk	1
7 oz	Tuna	200 g / 7 oz
4	Anchovies	4
2 tsp	Capers	2 tsp
1	Hard-cooked (boiled) egg yolk	1
1 tbsp	Vegetable oil	1 tbsp
⅔ cup	Consommé	150 ml / ¼ pint
1	Lemon	1

1. Simmer veal for 2 hours in salted water with carrot, onion and celery. Leave to cool in the liquid taking care it is completely covered.

2. Meanwhile prepare sauce. Drain tuna and put in a blender with anchovies and capers, blend on high speed for a few seconds. Put mixture into a bowl and add sieved egg yolk. Mix well, then beat in a little oil and the consommé, finally, add juice of lemon. The sauce should be light and frothy.

3. Drain veal well, slice thinly, lay on a serving dish and pour sauce over.

4. Cover dish with a sheet of cling wrap to prevent sauce discoloring and refrigerate for 24 hours before serving straight from the refrigerator.

Sage and black peppercorns (Veal Omelette with Sage)

Ossobuco milanese

Stewed Shin of Veal

	00:30		02:00

American	Ingredients	Metric/Imperial
6 x 3 in	Veal shin bones	6 x 7½ cm / 3 in
¼ cup	Flour	25 g / 1 oz
½ cup	Butter	100 g / 4 oz
1	Onion	1
1	Carrot	1
1	Celery stalk	1
2	Garlic cloves	2
3 – 4	Sprigs of marjoram	3 – 4
1	Bay leaf	1
1	Lemon	1
½ cup	Dry white wine	125 ml / 4 fl oz
6	Ripe or canned tomatoes	6
1 ¼ cups	Stock	300 ml / ½ pint
	Salt and pepper	
½ cup	Chopped parsley	6 tbsp

1. Ask the butcher to saw the shin of veal into the correctly sized pieces, dip in flour and shake off the excess.
2. Melt the butter over a medium heat in a large heavy pan and brown the veal shin on all sides. Remove onto a plate.
3. Chop the onion, carrot and celery into fine dice and crush the cloves of garlic. Cook in the pan over a low heat in the butter used for the veal for 5 minutes.
4. Stand the veal on its end, upright to prevent the marrow in the bone coming out. Add the marjoram and bay leaf with a small piece of lemon peel and the dry white wine. Cook on a high heat for 5 minutes.
5. Add the chopped tomatoes and stock, season well, bring to the boil, lower the heat, cover and cook for 1½ hours on a low heat. Add a little boiling water if the pan seems to be drying out during cooking.
6. Prepare the 'gremolata' which is an essential part of this dish by grating the remaining lemon peel finely, crush the other clove of garlic, mix with the lemon rind and the chopped parsley. When the dish is cooked, sprinkle with the lemon and parsley mixture.

Veau aux amandes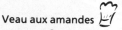
Veal with Almonds

🔪 00:10 00:35 🍲

American	Ingredients	Metric/Imperial
11 oz	Veal fillet	300 g / 11 oz
2 cups	Shelled almonds	275 g / 10 oz
3 tbsp	Butter	40 g / 1½ oz
¼ tsp	Chopped sage	¼ tsp
1 tsp	Cornstarch (cornflour)	1 tsp
⅔ cup	Dry white wine	150 ml / ¼ pint
	Salt and pepper	
¼ tsp	Curry powder	¼ tsp
1½ cups	Italian rice	300 g / 11 oz

1. Preheat oven to 400°F / 200°C / Gas Mark 6. Grease a large piece of foil and place on a baking sheet.
2. Dice veal, blanch almonds and mix the two together. Heat butter and sauté meat and almonds for 5 minutes with sage.
3. Blend cornstarch (cornflour) with wine and add to pan, stirring. Season with salt and pepper and a pinch of curry powder. Leave to simmer over a low heat.
4. Meanwhile boil rice until just tender, pile onto foil, make a hollow in the centre and fill with meat mixture. Close foil and cook in the oven for 10 minutes. Serve very hot.

Pancetta di vitello ripiena
Stuffed Breast of Veal

🔪 00:25 02:00 to 02:30 🍲

American	Ingredients	Metric/Imperial
2 oz	Cooked ham	50 g / 2 oz
2 oz	Mortadella	50 g / 2 oz
¾ lb	Ground (minced) meat (left-overs will do)	350 g / 12 oz
3	Eggs	3
¼ cup	Grated parmesan cheese	25 g / 1 oz
	Salt and pepper	
2 lb	Breast of veal	1 kg / 2 lb
1	Onion	1
2	Carrots	2
2	Bay leaves	2
1	Bouquet garni	1

1. Chop the ham and mortadella and mix with the ground meat, eggs, parmesan, salt and pepper.
2. Stuff the breast of veal with this mixture and sew up firmly with coarse kitchen string.
3. Chop the vegetables and put into a large saucepan with the bay leaves and bouquet garni with plenty of water, add the veal, wrapped in a boiled muslin cloth. Cook for at least 2 hours.
4. Remove from the pan, drain and allow to cool before unwrapping and slicing.

Involtini alla sarda
Veal in Tomato Sauce

00:20   00:30

American	Ingredients	Metric/Imperial
1 ¼ lb	Veal (from the shoulder)	600 g / 1 ¼ lb
½ cup	Parmesan cheese	50 g / 2 oz
2 tsp	Sage, chopped	2 tsp
½ cup	Soft bread crumbs	25 g / 1 oz
1	Egg	1
¼ lb	Cooked ham	100 g / 4 oz
	Flour	
¼ cup	Butter	50 g / 2 oz
	Salt and pepper	
3 tbsp	Marsala	2 tbsp
3	Ripe tomatoes	3
1	Stock cube	1

1. Try to slice the meat in such a way that each piece is of uniform size and thickness, flatten thick slices by beating.
2. Grate cheese onto sage, mix with bread crumbs and egg and season. Lay a slice of cooked ham on each piece of meat and spread the mixture over. Roll and secure with a toothpick, then dip into flour.
3. Heat the butter in a frying pan, add more sage then brown the rolled meat. Sprinkle with salt, pepper and marsala.
4. Preheat the oven to 350°F / 180°C / Gas Mark 4.
5. Skin and deseed tomatoes, chop and put into saucepan with a little stock and season. Place the veal in a casserole, cover with tomato sauce and cook for 20 minutes in the oven.

Fagottini di banana
Stuffed Veal Olives with Banana

00:20   Serves 6   00:25

American	Ingredients	Metric/Imperial
12	Small slices of leg of veal	12
6	Small bananas	6
1	Lemon	1
	Salt and pepper	
1 tsp	Mixed herbs	1 tsp
¼ cup	Butter	50 g / 2 oz
¼ cup	White wine	50 ml / 2 fl oz
1 cup	Coffee (single) cream	225 ml / 8 fl oz
1 tbsp	Chopped parsley	1 tbsp

1. Beat the slices of veal thoroughly and spread on a wooden board.
2. Peel the bananas and put the flesh in a bowl with the lemon juice, a pinch of salt, pepper and mixed herbs. Mix well and spread the mixture on the slices of meat, roll them round the banana mixture and fasten them with toothpicks.

3. Cook the veal olives in a pan with the heated butter for 10 minutes, adding a little white wine and some cream from time to time.

4. Cook on a gentle heat for a further 15 minutes. Serve sprinkled with chopped parsley accompanied by a selection of freshly cooked vegetables.

Sage, nutmeg and rosemary

Polpettone di vitello

Veal Meatloaf in a Béchamel Sauce

	00:30		01:00	

American	Ingredients	Metric/Imperial
¾ lb	Ground (minced) veal	350 g / 12 oz
½ lb	Ricotta (curd cheese)	225 g / 8 oz
3	Eggs	3
⅓ cup	Grated parmesan cheese	40 g / 1 ½ oz
	Salt and pepper	
¼ tsp	Nutmeg	¼ tsp
½ cup	Butter	100 g / 4 oz
½ tsp	Chopped sage	½ tsp
½ tsp	Chopped rosemary	½ tsp
	Bread crumbs	
2 tbsp	Marsala	1 ½ tbsp
3 cups	Thin béchamel sauce	700 ml / 1 ¼ pints

1. Preheat the oven to 350°F / 180°C / Gas Mark 4.

2. Mix together in a bowl the veal, ricotta, 1 whole egg, 2 egg yolks and some of the parmesan; season with salt, pepper and a pinch of nutmeg.

3. Heat a little butter in a pan and add sage and rosemary, cook for 1 minute, pour into a small loaf pan (tin) coating the sides and bottom.

4. Shape the meat mixture into a loaf and coat with the bread crumbs and mold into the pan. Pour over the marsala, sprinkle with parmesan cheese and cook in a moderate oven for 1 hour.

5. Prepare the béchamel sauce making sure it is not too thick.

6. When the meatloaf is cooked, transfer it to a serving dish and allow it to cool before pouring the béchamel sauce over it, adding another liberal sprinkling of parmesan. To serve, cut into medium-sized slices and accompany with roast potatoes.

Cotolettine di vitello gratinate

Veal Cutlets au Gratin

00:20
Soaking time 01:00

00:25

American	Ingredients	Metric/Imperial
8	Small veal loin steaks (cutlets)	8
3 tbsp	White flour	2 tbsp
2	Eggs	2
1 cup	Bread crumbs	100 g / 4 oz
½ cup	Butter	100 g / 4 oz
8	Slices of ham	8
8	Slices of fontina cheese	8
½ tsp	Nutmeg	½ tsp
	Salt and pepper	

1. Beat the cutlets on either side, flour lightly and soak in beaten egg for 1 hour. Coat in bread crumbs, pat the crumbs with the flat of the hand.
2. Heat the butter in a pan and fry the meat until golden brown each side, drain on absorbent kitchen towels.
3. Cool the cutlets and arrange in an ovenproof dish, place a slice of raw ham, without the fat, and a very thin slice of fontina on each cutlet.
4. Preheat the oven to 425°F / 220°C / Gas Mark 7.
5. Sprinkle with nutmeg, pepper and salt, and dot with butter. Place in a hot oven for 15 minutes and serve as soon as the cheese has melted.

Noce di vitello arrosto

Roast Veal

00:15
Serves 6

01:20

American	Ingredients	Metric/Imperial
3¼ lb	Round roast (leg) of veal	1.5 kg / 3¼ lb
2	Garlic cloves	2
¼ lb	Bacon	100 g / 4 oz
¼ cup	Oil	50 ml / 2 fl oz
2 tbsp	Butter	25 g / 1 oz
1	Bunch of parsley	1
2	Sprigs of rosemary	2
	Salt and pepper	
2 cups	Dry red wine	450 ml / ¾ pint

1. Preheat the oven to 350°F / 180°C / Gas Mark 4.
2. Pierce the veal with a small sharp knife, and insert slivers of garlic and bacon. Heat the oil and butter in a casserole and on a high heat brown the meat on all sides.
3. Chop the parsley and rosemary and add to the pot together with salt, several twists of pepper and the red wine. Cover and cook in the oven for 1¼ hours adding a little warm water, only if necessary. When the meat is cooked, transfer it to a board and cut into thin slices. Arrange on a heated serving dish.
4. Add a little water to the juice in the casserole and heat through to loosen the residue; sieve the liquid, reheat and serve with the roast.

Frittura piccata prigioniera

Fillet of Veal 'Prigioniera'

00:15   00:15

American	Ingredients	Metric/Imperial
14 oz	Fillet of veal, in slices	400 g / 14 oz
	Flour	
2 tbsp	Butter	25 g / 1 oz
1 cup	Cream	225 ml / 8 fl oz
1	Lemon	1
3 tbsp	Marsala	2 tbsp
	Salt and pepper	

1. Cut thin slices of veal, beat well. Dip in flour, shake off excess.
2. Heat the butter in a large frying pan, fry meat on both sides over a medium heat then turn the heat low and add cream. The veal slices should remain a pinkish color.
3. Sprinkle with grated lemon rind, continue cooking, turning the veal gently and moistening with the marsala. Season with salt and pepper when cooking is finished. Arrange meat on a heated serving dish.
4. The cooking sauce should be smooth and creamy, serve poured over the meat. Garnish with slices of the lemon.

Hamburger fantasiosi

Rissoles with Ham

00:20   00:20

American	Ingredients	Metric/Imperial
1 lb	Ground (minced) veal	500 g / 1 lb
1	Egg yolk	1
¼ lb	Cooked ham, finely chopped	100 g / 4 oz
1 tbsp	Olive oil	1 tbsp
	Salt and pepper	
1	Red chilli pepper	1
	Flour	
	Oil for frying	

1. Put the ground (minced) meat, egg yolk, finely chopped ham into a large bowl, add olive oil and season with salt and pepper.
2. Deseed the red chilli pepper, chop and mix with other ingredients until all are thoroughly blended.
3. Dust the hands lightly with flour and shape the mixture into 4 flattish rissoles.
4. Either fry the rissoles in oil, cooking them for 3 minutes each side in hot fat to brown and then reducing the heat to low or medium to cook for another 7 minutes on each side. Or cook them under the broiler (grill). If broiling, turn them so that the rissoles brown on both sides.
5. Serve at once with rice and green salad.

Busecca

Tripe and Vegetables

	00:35		01:40	

American	Ingredients	Metric/Imperial
1 lb	Veal tripe	450 g / 1 lb
	Salt and pepper	
1	Potato	1
1	Celery stalk	1
1	Leek	1
1	Carrot	1
1	Onion	1
½	Savoy cabbage	½
¼ lb	Tomatoes	100 g / 4 oz
¼ lb	Green beans	100 g / 4 oz
¼ cup	Butter	50 g / 2 oz
2 oz	Bacon, chopped	50 g / 2 oz
2	Stock cubes	2
2 tbsp	Chopped parsley	1 ½ tbsp
½	Garlic clove	½
2	Sage leaves	2
1 cup	Grated parmesan cheese	100 g / 4 oz

1. Take the veal tripe, remove the fat, scrape and wash thoroughly. Place in boiling salted water and simmer for 20 minutes. Drain, cool slightly and cut it into strips.
2. Chop a large peeled potato, the celery heart, the leek, carrot, onion, cabbage, tomatoes and the beans very finely.
3. Heat the butter in a pan, add the chopped bacon and cook for 5 minutes.
4. Prepare a stock with 2½ cups [600 ml / 1 pint] water and the cubes and put it on one side.
5. Mix the tripe with bacon. Then add the stock and cook for a further 40 minutes.
6. Add the vegetables and cook for another 20 minutes.
7. Add finely chopped parsley together with the crushed garlic, sage leaves and a good twist of pepper. Sprinkle with plenty of grated parmesan. Cook for a further 10 minutes or until the vegetables are cooked and taste for seasoning. Serve very hot.

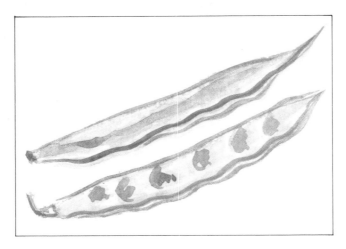

Trippa alla contadina

Tripe Peasant-Style

| | 00:10 | | 02:10 | |

American	Ingredients	Metric/Imperial
1¾ lb	Veal tripe	800 g / 1¾ lb
¼ lb	Parma ham	100 g / 4 oz
1	Small onion	1
3	Celery stalks	3
1	Carrot	1
1	Sprig of parsley	1
⅓ cup	Butter	75 g / 3 oz
1 tbsp	Tomato purée	1 tbsp
1	Clove	1
¼ tsp	Nutmeg	¼ tsp
	Salt and pepper	
4	Slices of white bread	4
½ cup	Grated parmesan cheese	50 g / 2 oz

1. Wash tripe very thoroughly in several changes of water, blanch and cut into narrow strips.
2. Chop ham, onion, celery, carrot and parsley. Heat half the butter and fry ham and vegetables for 2-3 minutes. Add tripe and fry a further few minutes, stirring constantly.
3. Dissolve tomato purée in a little hot water, add to pot together with clove and a pinch of nutmeg. Cover and simmer for about 2 hours, adding salt and pepper towards the end.
4. Heat remaining butter and fry bread slices. Put one slice in each soup bowl, pile with tripe and vegetables and a good sprinkling of freshly grated parmesan.

Frittata di cervella e ricotta

Brains and Ricotta Omelette

| | 00:10 | | 00:10 | |

American	Ingredients	Metric/Imperial
½	Calf's brain	½
	Salt and pepper	
7 oz	Ricotta	200 g / 7 oz
6	Eggs	6
½ cup	Oil	125 ml / 4 fl oz

1. Wash and skin the brains, bring to the boil in salted water and simmer for 10 minutes, drain them and allow to cool. Cut into small pieces or blend.
2. Sieve the ricotta, add the brains and beat or blend to obtain a smooth mixture. Beat the eggs in a bowl, add a pinch of salt and pepper, then little by little mix in the brains and ricotta mixture. Beat as though making an ordinary omelette mixture.
3. Heat the oil in an iron frying pan, pour in the mixture and cook like a normal omelette. To cook the other side, slip the omelette on to a plate and return to the pan upside down. Lay on a serving dish and slice. Serve with salad or buttered spinach.

Rognone e riso in umido

Braised Calves' Kidneys with Rice

⌧▷ 00:40   00:35 ⌔

American	Ingredients	Metric/Imperial
1 lb	Calves' kidneys	500 g / 1 lb
3 tbsp	Vinegar	2 tbsp
½ cup	Butter	100 g / 4 oz
	Salt and pepper	
½ cup	Dry white wine	125 ml / 4 fl oz
2	Garlic cloves	2
1 tbsp	Chopped parsley	1 tbsp
1 tsp	Rosemary	1 tsp
1 cup	Rice	200 g / 7 oz

1. Slice the kidneys finely and remove all the fat; soak in vinegar and water for about 30 minutes.
2. Melt the butter in a heavy pan and when it is hot add the kidneys, brown and season.
3. Add the wine and allow it to evaporate, continue to cook for 15 minutes over a low heat.
4. Crush the garlic, chop the parsley and rosemary and mix.
5. Cook the rice in salted water until 'al dente', drain.
6. Place the kidneys in the middle of a heated serving dish, sprinkle with the garlic and rosemary mixture, surround with the rice and serve.

Fegato all'italiana in salsa

Italian-Style Liver in Sauce

⌧▷ 00:15   00:20 ⌔

American	Ingredients	Metric/Imperial
1 lb	Calf's liver	500 g / 1 lb
	Flour	
	Salt and pepper	
¼ cup	Butter	50 g / 2 oz
3 oz	Raw ham	75 g / 3 oz
1	Small onion	1
2 or 3	Sage leaves	2 or 3
1	Bunch of parsley	1
2 tsp	Cornstarch (cornflour)	2 tsp
1	Stock cube	1
3 tbsp	Marsala	2 tbsp

1. Cut the liver into slices and dip in seasoned flour, shake off excess.
2. Heat the butter, add the liver and fry for 5 minutes. Remove the slices and keep warm.
3. Chop the ham, a small onion, a few sage leaves and a bunch of parsley, and fry them in the same butter over a low heat for 6 minutes.

4. Add cornstarch dissolved in 1¼ cups [300 ml / ½ pint] stock with a small glass of marsala, and simmer for 10 minutes. Put the liver back in the sauce for a few minutes. Serve hot, adding seasoning at the last minute.

Rognoni di vitello

Kidneys in Cream Sauce

	00:20		00:15	

American	Ingredients	Metric/Imperial
1½ lb	Veal or lamb's kidneys	700 g / 1½ lb
3 tbsp	Flour	2 tbsp
½ cup	Butter	50 g / 2 oz
2	Medium-sized onions	2
1	Small garlic clove	1
¼ tsp	Thyme	¼ tsp
½ cup	Red wine	125 ml / 4 fl oz
	Salt and pepper	
½ cup	Cream	6 tbsp
12	Slices small crusty loaf	12
	Oil for frying	
1 tbsp	Chopped parsley	1 tbsp
1 tsp	Juniper berries	1 tsp

1. Prepare the kidneys by removing the skin and the core.
2. Flour the kidneys and fry in butter over medium heat. Add chopped onion, garlic and thyme. Cook for 6 minutes.
3. Add the wine, raise the heat for 2 minutes. Reduce the heat to low and stir in cream and juniper berries. Cook for a further 8 minutes and season well.
4. Fry the sliced bread in oil until crisp, drain on absorbent kitchen towels. Wash the parsley, chop finely and add to the kidneys.
5. Pour the kidneys into a heated serving dish, surround with fried bread and garnish with sprigs of parsley.

Parsley, garlic and juniper berries

BUYING AND COOKING BEEF

	Cooking methods
American cuts to choose Wedgebone, flatbone, pinbone, porterhouse, t-bone, rib, rump	roast, broil (grill) or fry
Steaks from these cuts Short plate, brisket, chuck, short ribs, foreshank	braise or pot roast
chuck, neck, hand shank (round), bottom round, heel of round, brisket, oxtail	stew
British cuts to choose Aitchbone, fillet, forerib, back, middle rib and wing rib, rump, sirloin, topside	**Cooking methods** roast
Steaks from these cuts Aitchbone, top rump, leg, skirt, silverside, brisket, back and top rib, flank, topside, chuck, bladebone	braise, stew
clod or neck, shin, oxtail	stew

Polpettine alla béchamel

Beef Rissoles

	00:30	00:06 each batch

American	Ingredients	Metric/Imperial
1½ cups	Ground (minced) beef (cooked left-overs can be used)	350 g / 12 oz
2	Eggs	2
1¼ cups	Thick béchemal	300 ml / ½ pint
2 tbsp	Grated parmesan cheese	1½ tbsp
¼ tsp	Nutmeg	¼ tsp
	Salt and pepper	
2 tbsp	Flour	15 g / ½ oz
	Bread crumbs	
1 cup	Oil	225 ml / 8 fl oz
	Lemon slices	

1. Combine the meat, eggs, béchamel sauce, parmesan, nutmeg, salt and pepper. Flour the hands and shape the rissoles into small, slightly flattened rounds. If time permits, chill for 30 minutes before coating.
2. Coat with bread crumbs and fry over a brisk heat in plenty of oil. Drain on paper towels to absorb the excess oil. Transfer to a warm serving dish and garnish with lemon slices.

Sciuscieddu siciliano

Baked Meatballs with Ricotta

	00:20	01:00

American	Ingredients	Metric/Imperial
11 oz	Ground (minced) meat	300 g / 11 oz
1 tbsp	Chopped parsley	1 tbsp
3	Eggs	3
1 cup	Grated parmesan cheese	100 g / 4 oz
1	Bread roll	1
1 quart	Stock	1 litre / 1¾ pints
1½ lb	Ricotta cheese	700 g / 1½ lb

1. Preheat oven to 400°F / 200°C / Gaş Mark 6. Butter an ovenproof serving dish.
2. Mix together ground (minced) meat, chopped parsley, 1 egg, some parmesan and the roll soaked in milk. Season and shape into meatballs; simmer in stock for 20 minutes.
3. Combine ricotta with remaining 2 eggs and rest of the parmesan. Place alternate layers of ricotta mixture and meatballs in the dish ending with a layer of meatballs; pour over a little stock, cover and cook in the oven for about 40 minutes.

Bollito freddo alla ligure

Ligurian Cold Boiled Beef

	00:30 Serves 6	03:00

American	Ingredients	Metric/Imperial
3 ¼ lb	Beef brisket	1.5 kg / 3 ¼ lb
1	Carrot	1
1	Celery stalk	1
1	Onion	1
1	Bunch of parsley	1
6	Hard crackers (biscuits)	6
1 cup	Red wine	225 ml / 8 fl oz
¼ cup	Vegetable oil	50 ml / 2 fl oz
2 tbsp	Vinegar	1 ½ tbsp
4	Anchovies	4
1 tbsp	Capers	1 tbsp
Scant ¼ cup	Olive oil	3 tbsp
1 tbsp	Mustard	1 tbsp
1	Hard-cooked (boiled egg)	1
	Salt and pepper	
	Pickled onions	
	Gherkins	

1. Put the rolled beef in a saucepan with the peeled carrot, celery, onion and a bunch of parsley, cover with water, bring to the boil and simmer for about 3 hours (or 40 minutes in a pressure cooker). When cooked, drain the beef from the stock (use stock for soup) and cool.

2. Cut the beef into small pieces and put it in a large pot. Crumble the hard crackers (biscuits) over and cover with strong red wine.

3. Beat the oil and vinegar together in a cup as for making a salad dressing, and pour over the meat. Return to the heat and simmer slowly until all the liquid has reduced; then cool.

4. Prepare a sauce by chopping and pounding (or make in a blender or food processor) the desalted and boned anchovy fillets and the capers, and dilute with olive oil. Add mustard, chopped hard-cooked (boiled) egg, salt and pepper and blend until you obtain a smooth sauce.

5. Remove the meat from the pot, place it on a serving dish and cover it with the sauce; allow to stand in a cool place but do not chill. Serve the beef decorated with pickled onions and gherkins.

Roast beef classico

Sirloin of Beef Pan-Roasted

	00:15	00:32

American	Ingredients	Metric/Imperial
3¼ lb	Beef tip (sirloin) joint	1.5 kg / 3¼ lb
	Salt and pepper	
1 cup	Olive oil	225 ml / 8 fl oz
1	Sprig of rosemary	1
2	Garlic cloves	2

1. Wipe the meat well, roll and tie with string or ask the butcher to do this for you. Season with salt and pepper.
2. Put the olive oil into a heavy frying pan with rosemary and the garlic, remove these as soon as they have colored.
3. When the oil begins to smoke, add the meat and turn continuously for exactly 30 minutes, turn heat down to moderate after 5 minutes each side.
4. Remove and stand between two plates with a weight on top. Leave for 10 minutes to allow the juices to drain out, collect and return juice to the pan. Heat gently to boiling point and tip into a sauceboat.
5. Remove the string from the joint, carve into wafer-thin slices and serve immediately.

Arrosto vecchio Piemonte

'Old Piedmont' Roast

	00:30	00:40

American	Ingredients	Metric/Imperial
¾ lb	Shortcrust pastry	350 g / 12 oz
1¼ lb	Sirloin beef, in a single slice	600 g / 1¼ lb
7 oz	Prague ham	200 g / 7 oz
¼ cup	Béchamel sauce	50 ml / 2 fl oz
1 tsp	Mixed spice	1 tsp
½ cup	Butter	100 g / 4 oz
2 or 3	Sage leaves	2 or 3

1. Preheat the oven to 350°F / 180°C / Gas Mark 4.
2. Roll out the pastry and lay the well beaten slice of beef on top. Put the ham on top of the meat, spread over a little béchamel and sprinkle with spice. Roll up the pastry with the meat filling. Damp and press the edges so that they are well sealed.
3. Place in a buttered baking pan, pour over the melted butter and add a few sage leaves. Put in a preheated oven and cook for 40 minutes, occasionally turning the roll carefully until it has taken on a good rosy color. If the cooking juice becomes too dry, add a little more butter.
4. Remove from the oven, let it cool, then cut into thick slices, putting two or three slices on each plate. Put the plates in a hot oven for a few moments before serving.

Costata alla campagnola

Country Sirloin

This is a stew of country origin, where the pot in the centre of the table invites drinking and lively conversation.

00:10 01:00 to 01:30

American	Ingredients	Metric/Imperial
Scant ¼ cup	Vegetable oil	3 tbsp
¼ cup	Butter	50 g / 2 oz
1	Onion	1
1	Bunch of parsley	1
1	Celery stalk	1
1	Carrot	1
3 lb	Piece of sirloin	1 kg / 3 lb
	Salt and pepper	
⅔ cup	Dry white wine	150 ml / ¼ pint
1	Stock cube	1

1. Put oil and butter into a high sided heatproof pan, prepare and chop the vegetables; add the sirloin, boned and rolled. Brown on all sides.
2. Season with salt and pepper and moisten with good dry white wine. Add about 1 cup [225 ml / 8 fl oz] of stock made from a cube and boil on a vigorous heat until the wine and stock are almost absorbed.
3. Reduce the heat and cook for about 1 hour, turning the meat from time to time and, if necessary, adding more stock.
4. When the meat is cooked, place on a dish, return the pan to the heat with the strained sauce, add a little more white wine and reduce the heat to low. Cut the meat into thick slices, put it back into the sauce and serve immediately in the pan or casserole.

Roast beef allo champagne

Rib of Beef Cooked in Champagne

00:10 00:20
Standing time 00:20

American	Ingredients	Metric/Imperial
2 lb	Rolled rib of beef	1 kg / 2 lb
½ cup	Butter	100 g / 4 oz
Scant ¼ cup	Oil	3 tbsp
2 cups	Dry champagne	450 ml / ¾ pint
	Pepper	
1	Stock cube	1

1. Have bones removed by the butcher and the meat rolled. Wipe the meat and remove any membranes.
2. Melt the butter in a saucepan, then add the oil and brown the meat, turning continually for the first 10 minutes. Pour the champagne (other sparkling wine can be used) over the meat and continue to cook for a further 5 minutes, then add a few twists of pepper and the stock cube dissolved in ⅔ cup [150 ml / ¼ pint] hot water.

3. After 18 minutes, transfer the beef to a dish, cover and place a weight on top. Leave for 20 minutes to allow some of the juices to run out. Tip these back into the saucepan, reduce if necessary and serve separately. Carve a few slices from the joint and arrange on a heated serving dish together with the uncut portion. Surround the meat with fried or baked potatoes, warm through for a few seconds in a hot oven and serve.

Bocconcini di manzo piccanti

Spicy Beef Bouchées

🥄 00:25   01:20 🍲

American	Ingredients	Metric/Imperial
2	Large onions	2
¼ cup	Vegetable oil	50 ml / 2 fl oz
¼ cup	Butter	50 g / 2 oz
1½ lb	Lean braising beef	700 g / 1½ lb
	Salt and pepper	
½ tsp	Paprika	½ tsp
1	Beef stock cube	1
15 oz	Peeled plum tomatoes	425 g / 15 oz
2 or 3	Potatoes	2 or 3
1 tbsp	Chopped parsley	1 tbsp

1. Cut the onions into rings. Heat the oil and butter in a pan over a low heat and cook the onions for 6 minutes.
2. Cut meat into cubes and add to the onions, which can be pushed to the side of the pan, with salt and a generous sprinkling of paprika. Raise the heat and stir for a further 5 minutes.
3. Add 2½ cups [600 ml / 1 pint] water with the stock cube dissolved in it, the tomatoes and the peeled, thickly sliced potatoes. Bring to the boil and simmer for 1 hour. Test meat to make sure it is tender.
4. Taste and adjust the seasoning, add more paprika if necessary. Remove from the heat and leave covered for 10 minutes. Stir round with a wooden spoon to break down the potato and thicken the beef mixture. Sprinkle with parsley. Serve hot, with boiled rice or crusty bread.

Bollito misto

Boiled Mixed Meats

This famous dish comes from Piedmont and is ideal for a large family party.

01:00
Serves 10
Plus 06:00 soaking

03:00 to 04:00

American	Ingredients	Metric/Imperial
2 lb	Short ribs of beef	1 kg / 2 lb
2 lb	Bottom round of beef	1 kg / 2 lb
1 lb	Breast of veal, trimmed	450 g / 1 lb
1½ lb	Shoulder of lamb	700 g / 1½ lb
1	Calf's foot	1
½ lb	Belly of pork, trimmed	225 g / 8 oz
½ lb	Sausage	225 g / 8 oz
1	Ox tongue, soaked for 6 hours	1
1	Onion	1
2	Cloves	2
1	Garlic clove	1
2	Tomatoes, peeled and drained	2
2	Sprigs of parsley	2
8	Sprigs of thyme	8
2	Bay leaves	2
	Salt and pepper	
1 lb	New potatoes	450 g / 1 lb
24	Small onions	24
1 lb	Cabbage	450 g / 1 lb
1 lb	Zucchini (courgette)	450 g / 1 lb
1 lb	Carrots	450 g / 1 lb
1 lb	Green beans	450 g / 1 lb
1 quart	Béchamel sauce	1 litre / 1¾ pints
2½ cups	Green sauce	600 ml / 1 pint

1. Place all the meat in a very large pot with the soaked tongue, do not add the sausage at this stage. Cover with cold water, add the onion stuck with cloves, garlic, tomatoes, parsley, thyme and bay leaves.

2. Bring to the boil slowly and remove the scum as it rises to the surface.

3. Season with salt and pepper and simmer for 2-3 hours. Remove each joint of meat as it becomes tender; the veal and lamb will be cooked first. Add the sausage. Continue to skim the fat and scum from the surface as cooking progresses. The tongue will take longest to cook; drain it and skin when cooked.

4. At the end of 2½ hours start cooking the vegetables in a little stock from the meat or water, as preferred. Make sure that the vegetables are crisp. Keep warm.

5. Make the béchamel sauce with half meat broth and half and half milk and cream. Make the green sauce.

6. Carve the meats on a large heated serving platter and keep warm covered with foil in a low oven, adding a little meat stock from time to time. Garnish with parsley sprigs.

7. Serve the cooked vegetables on several platters covered with the béchamel sauce. Serve the green sauce separately.

Magatello in salsa del Don

Beef in 'Don' Sauce

| | 00:30 | | 00:00 | |

American	Ingredients	Metric/Imperial
1 ¼ lb	Fillet steak	600 g / 1 ¼ lb
Sauce		
2	Egg yolks	2
¼ cup	Oil	50 ml / 2 fl oz
1	Lemon	1
3 tbsp	Chopped black olives	2 tbsp
½ tsp	Anchovy paste	½ tsp
1 tsp	Mustard	1 tsp
	Salt and pepper	

1. Have your butcher slice the beef very thinly (with the meat slicer) and then arrange the slices on a serving dish.
2. Put the egg yolks into the blender, switch on, add oil gradually and when you can see that it is well beaten, add the lemon juice, the chopped black olives, the anchovy paste, the mustard, and salt and pepper to taste. Blend again to obtain a smooth sauce. Transfer to a bowl and place in the refrigerator for 30 minutes.
3. Cover the fillet of beef with the sauce and garnish the dish with black olives.

Involtini tirolesi

Tyrolean Beef Potatoes

| | 00:20 | | 01:00 | |

American	Ingredients	Metric/Imperial
8	Slices of fillet beef	8
	Salt	
¼ lb	Cooked ham	100 g / 4 oz
6	Würstel (frankfurters)	6
¼ cup	Butter	50 g / 2 oz
¼ cup	Dry white wine	50 ml / 2 fl oz
½	Stock cube	½
1 ¼ cups	Aspic	300 ml / ½ pint
	Pickles	

1. Have the meat sliced fairly thin, beat slices with a cutlet bat.
2. Salt the slices and place on each, 1 slice of cooked ham and half a frankfurter, scalded, with the skin removed. Roll the meat around the sausage to form an olive.
3. Heat the butter in a large frying pan and fry the olives until they are well browned. Moisten with white wine and evaporate it quickly. Add 1 ¼ cups [300 ml / ½ pint] of hot water with half a stock cube crumbled in and continue cooking on a low heat for about 45 minutes.
4. Prepare the aspic following the instructions on the packet and allow to cool, using cooking juices as part of the liquid. Drain the beef olives, arrange in an oval dish and decorate the space between the olives with pickles. Pour on the aspic, let it cool and place in the refrigerator. Serve with a salad.

Filetto en croûte

Fillet en Croûte

	01:00		00:45

American	Ingredients	Metric/Imperial
2	Carrots	2
2	Onions	2
1	Sprig of rosemary	1
½ cup	Butter	100 g / 4 oz
	Salt and pepper	
2 oz	Fat bacon	50 g / 2 oz
2 lb	Fillet steak	1 kg / 2 lb
2 oz	Chicken livers	50 g / 2 oz
1½ oz	Cooked ham	40 g / 1½ oz
2	Eggs	2
3 tbsp	Brandy	2 tbsp
1 (8 oz)	Packet of pastry	1 (225 g / 8 oz)

1. Preheat oven to 425°F / 220°C / Gas Mark 7.

2. Finely chop the prepared carrots and onions, fry them with rosemary in a little butter, and season with salt and pepper.

3. Slice the bacon very thinly and rub the fillet with it.

4. Grind (mince) the chicken livers and the ham finely or put through a food processor to obtain a fine mixture. Add to the carrots and onions with the egg and brandy. Season the fillet with salt and pepper and spread prepared sauce on top.

5. Roll the flaky or puff pastry out on the table, place the fillet on top and close it, pressing the edges down well so that it is completely sealed. Make small holes in the pastry with a fork, and finally brush it with the beaten egg.

6. Put the fillet wrapped in pastry in an oven pan and place in the oven for 15 minutes. Reduce the temperature to 325°F / 170°C / Gas Mark 3 for about 30 minutes.

7. Remove from the oven, allow to cool a little, cut the meat into slices and arrange it on a serving dish.

Cotolette di trita alla milanese

Milanese Meat Cutlets

00:30
Chilling time 01:00

01:30

American	Ingredients	Metric/Imperial
1	Inside of bread roll	1
Scant ¼ cup	Milk	3 tbsp
1 lb	Ground (minced) meat (can be left-overs)	500 g / 1 lb
3	Eggs	3
1 tbsp	Grated parmesan cheese	1 tbsp
	Salt and pepper	
	Flour	
	Bread crumbs	
⅓ cup	Oil	75 ml / 3 fl oz
2 tbsp	Butter	25 g / 1 oz
1 tbsp	Chopped parsley	1 tbsp
2	Lemons	2

1. Soak the bread in warm milk, squeeze, then put through the grinder (mincer) together with the meat (if the meat you are using is already minced, put it through the grinder a second time), add 2 eggs, a little grated parmesan, salt and pepper. If the mixture is too soft add a few bread crumbs.
2. Shape into cutlets, flatten them and chill in the refrigerator for 1 hour.
3. Coat the cutlets in flour, the remaining egg and the bread crumbs. Heat oil and butter on a moderate heat and fry for 5 minutes on each side. Serve with a sprinkling of chopped parsley and lemon slices.

Stufatino annegato

Spicy Beef Stew

00:20

02:15

American	Ingredients	Metric/Imperial
1½ lb	Beef (flank)	600 g / 1½ lb
7 oz	Parma ham (single piece)	200 g / 7 oz
11 oz	Peas	300 g / 11 oz
1	Onion	1
2	Cloves	2
⅔ cup	Dry white wine	150 ml / ¼ pint
1 quart	Stock	1 litre / 1¾ pints
¼ tsp	Curry powder	¼ tsp
	Salt and pepper	

1. Cut meat into 1 in / 2.5 cm cubes, trimming away fat. Put beef into a large saucepan, cube parma ham and pile, with the peas, around the meat; stud onion with cloves and add to pan. Pour over wine and cook over medium heat for 10 minutes.
2. Add stock and a pinch of curry powder. Cover and simmer for about 2 hours.
3. Just before serving add salt and pepper and serve hot.

35

Filetto in salsa

Beef Fillet in Sauce

00:25   00:20 to 00:30

American	Ingredients	Metric/Imperial
1 ½ lb	Fillet beef	700 g / 1 ½ lb
1	Garlic clove	1
1 oz	Bacon	25 g / 1 oz
2 tbsp	Chopped parsley	1 ½ tbsp
3 tbsp	Butter	40 g / 1 ½ oz
1 tsp	Curry powder	1 tsp
½ cup	Cream	125 ml / 4 fl oz

1. Spread out and beat the open fillet to form a single slice, lay on top a crushed clove of garlic, a little bacon cut into strips and a little chopped parsley. Roll up the slice of meat, then sew it with white thread or secure with toothpicks.
2. Melt a little butter in a frying pan and cook for about 20 minutes, finally adding the curry powder, the parsley and a little cream. Place on a heated serving dish and serve very hot.

Polpettone fantastico

Decorated Meatloaf

00:45   03:10

American	Ingredients	Metric/Imperial
2 ½ cups	Ground (minced) beef or other meat	600 g / 1 ¼ lb
5 oz	Cooked ham	150 g / 5 oz
¼ lb	Italian sausage	100 g / 4 oz
	Chopped parsley	
4	Celery stalks	4
6	Eggs	6
¼ cup	Grated parmesan cheese	25 g / 1 oz
	Salt and pepper	
1 tbsp	Bread crumbs	1 tbsp
4	Carrots	4
1	Onion	1
1	Bouquet garni	1

1. Put the ground (minced) meat and ham into a large bowl with the ground (minced) sausage, some chopped parsley, 2 stalks of celery, finely chopped, 4 eggs and the parmesan cheese. Season with salt and pepper. Mix all these ingredients thoroughly until they form a sticky mixture, adding bread crumbs if the mixture is too wet. Use the food processor for this if possible.
2. Hard-cook (boil) 2 eggs and cool under running cold water, remove the shells.
3. Soak and wring out a clean white cloth and place the mixture on it, pressing it into the shape of a large salame sausage. Wash and peel 2 medium-sized carrots and lay them along the sides of a meatloaf; place one hard-cooked (boiled) egg at each end. Press these well into the meat so that they are

covered, then wrap the cloth around the whole and sew up with white thread.

4. In a large saucepan bring 2 quarts [2 litres / 3½ pints] of water to the boil, add the onion, remaining celery and carrot. Immerse the meatloaf and cook for 3 hours over a medium heat. When quite cold, unwrap and cut into slices.

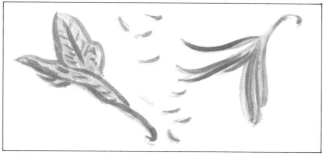

Sage, fennel seeds and rosemary

Involtini ai due sapori

Beef Olives with Two Different Flavors

🔪	01:00	01:00 🍲
American	**Ingredients**	**Metric/Imperial**
11 oz	Round (top rump) steak, sliced	300 g / 11 oz
11 oz	Loin of pork, sliced	300 g / 11 oz
¼ lb	Bacon	100 g / 4 oz
8	Sage leaves	8
2 oz	Gruyère cheese	50 g / 2 oz
¼ lb	Cooked ham	100 g / 4 oz
	Fennel seeds	
¼ cup	Butter	50 g / 2 oz
1 tbsp	Oil	1 tbsp
1	Sprig of rosemary	1
1	Sprig of sage	1
¼ cup	Dry white wine	50 ml / 2 fl oz
1	Stock cube	1
1 tsp	Cornstarch (cornflour)	1 tsp

1. Beat the slices of steak and pork until they are thin and flat, taking care not to tear them, remove any fat or gristle.

2. On each piece of steak place a slice of bacon, a sage leaf and a small strip of gruyère.

3. On each piece of the pork place a slice of ham, a sage leaf and 2 fennel seeds. Roll up each parcel and secure with a toothpick.

4. Melt some butter and oil in a heavy pan, add a sprig each of rosemary and sage. Place the olives in the pan and fry, browning them well on all sides. Add dry white wine and a twist of pepper and allow to cook slowly for 30-40 minutes, keeping the meat moist with water in which a stock cube has been dissolved. Remove the meat on to a heated serving dish.

5. Place the pan over the heat, add 2-3 tablespoons of water and warm through very gently. Thicken the cooking liquid with cornstarch and serve with a potato purée.

Stracotto di manzo

Stewed Beef

	00:10		01:00

American	Ingredients	Metric/Imperial
1	Onion	1
1	Carrot	1
¼ cup	Butter	50 g / 2 oz
1 lb	Sirloin beef, boned and rolled	500 g / 1 lb
3 tbsp	Wine vinegar	2 tbsp
1 cup	Milk	225 ml / 8 fl oz
1 cup	Whipping (double) cream	225 ml / 8 fl oz
	Salt	

1. Peel and quarter onion, coarsely chop the carrot.
2. Heat butter in a heavy pan and, when foaming, add beef joint and brown meat all over. Add carrot and onion to pan and cook for 1-2 minutes.
3. Pour over vinegar and simmer for 5 minutes. Add milk and cream, cover and simmer for about 1 hour, adding more milk if required. Season with salt.
4. Remove joint, discard string, slice thickly and arrange on a hot serving plate. Pour sauce through a sieve over the meat and serve at once.

Bocconcini alla lombarda

Lombardy Bouchées

	00:25		00:40

American	Ingredients	Metric/Imperial
1 ½ lb	Rumpsteak	800 g / 1 ½ lb
1	Egg	1
	Salt and pepper	
1 cup	Bread crumbs	100 g / 4 oz
¼ cup	Vegetable oil	50 ml / 2 fl oz
2	Garlic cloves	2
1 cup	Cream	225 ml / 8 fl oz
¼ tsp	Nutmeg	¼ tsp
1 tbsp	Chopped parsley	1 tbsp

1. Cut the beef into strips, trimming away gristle and fat. Coat in the egg beaten with a little salt and then in the bread crumbs, as for cutlets.
2. Heat the oil and fry meat on both sides. Drain the beef strips and keep warm in a covered dish.
3. Put the crushed garlic in a casserole (not a metal one) with a small amount of frying oil, and as soon as the garlic starts to brown add the pieces of meat and pour in all the cream. Turn down the heat and stir, otherwise the cream will burn, season with salt and pepper.
4. Stir from time to time and, turning the meat, carry on cooking for a further 20 minutes on an extremely low heat. Before serving sprinkle with nutmeg and chopped parsley. Serve accompanied by boiled rice.

Brasato all'acciuga

Braised Beef with Anchovies

	00:15		02:00

American	Ingredients	Metric/Imperial
3	Slices of bacon	3
Scant ¼ cup	Vegetable oil	3 tbsp
1¾ lb	Chuck steak	800 g / 1¾ lb
	Salt and pepper	
½ tsp	Nutmeg	½ tsp
3	Anchovies, desalted and boned	3
1	Stock cube	1
2 or 3	Sprigs of parsley	2 or 3

1. Chop the bacon into small pieces and put it in a pan with the heated oil, brown slightly, then add the piece of meat, season with salt and pepper and sprinkle with nutmeg. When the meat is browned on all sides, lower the flame and begin cooking.
2. Add the chopped anchovies and the parsley, mix in the 2½ cups [600 ml / 1 pint] stock made from the cube, cover and cook on a slow heat for about 2 hours.
3. Turn from time to time, add more stock if necessary, and check seasoning. Serve the meat in slices with boiled rice.

Pilau sardo

Beef with Rice

	00:10		02:00

American	Ingredients	Metric/Imperial
2 lb	Joint of beef brisket	1 kg / 2 lb
⅔ cup	Oil	150 ml / ¼ pint
¼ tsp	Chopped thyme	¼ tsp
¼ tsp	Chopped bay leaf	¼ tsp
¼ tsp	Chopped rosemary	¼ tsp
¼ tsp	Garlic powder	¼ tsp
½ cup	Dry white wine	125 ml / 4 fl oz
Scant 2 cups	Stock	450 ml / ¾ pint
1	Egg yolk	1
1	Lemon	1
	Salt and pepper	

1. Put the meat into a saucepan containing heated oil, add a ¼ teaspoon of thyme, bay, rosemary and garlic powder; pour over the wine gradually; when this has evaporated completely, add the stock. Cover and simmer until the meat is tender, which will take 1½-2 hours.
2. Remove from the pan. Strain the cooking juices, mix in the egg yolk and lemon juice and taste for seasoning.
3. Slice the meat, pour over some gravy, serving the rest in a sauceboat and serve with boiled rice.

Manzo brasato al barolo

Beef in Red Wine

00:30   02:00

American	Ingredients	Metric/Imperial
1½ oz	Cooked ham	40 g / 1½ oz
3 lb	Brisket beef	1.4 kg / 3 lb
2 tbsp	Lard	25 g / 1 oz
Scant ¼ cup	Oil	3 tbsp
3 tbsp	Butter	40 g / 1½ oz
	Salt and pepper	
1 (70 cl)	Bottle of Barolo wine	1 (70 cl)
2	Carrots	2
2	Onions	2
4	Celery stalks	4
1	Stock cube	1
	Potatoes	

1. Dice the ham and insert it around the outside of the beef. Rub all over with lard.
2. Choose a heavy saucepan with a lid, add the oil and butter, allow to bubble and then lay the meat in the pan. Season with salt and pepper, pour in the wine, which should cover the meat completely.
3. Prepare and chop the vegetables, and when most of the wine has evaporated add them to the saucepan together with a stock cube made up with 2½ cups [600 ml / 1 pint] of water. Cover and braise for at least 2 hours.
4. Prepare boiled potatoes to serve with the meat. Remove the beef to a carving board, slice it and arrange on a heated dish, surrounded by the vegetables. Serve hot with cooking liquid in a sauceboat.

Costata di manzo alla griglia

Grilled Sirloin Steak

00:30   00:12
Marinating time 00:30

American	Ingredients	Metric/Imperial
½ cup	Olive oil	125 ml / 4 fl oz
¼ tsp	Chopped sage	¼ tsp
½ tsp	Chopped mint	½ tsp
¼ tsp	Chopped tarragon	¼ tsp
	Salt and pepper	
4	Sirloin steaks	4
2	Tomatoes	2
1	Sweet pepper	1
Scant ¼ cup	Oil	3 tbsp

1. Pour olive oil into a bowl and add the sage, mint and tarragon leaves, washed and finely chopped, season with salt and pepper and marinate steaks for about 30 minutes.
2. Wash and halve the tomatoes and the deseeded peppers. Heat the oil in a frying pan and cook the tomatoes and peppers. Remove and keep warm in a heated dish.
3. Raise the heat, add the steaks drained of their marinade.

Cook for just 4 minutes on each side, as the meat should remain quite red. Arrange the steaks on the heated serving dish, pour over a little of the oil flavored with the herbs, and garnish with the vegetables.

Filetto all'uva

Fillet Steak with Grapes

00:30   00:45

American	Ingredients	Metric/Imperial
1¾ lb	Fillet steak	800 g / 1¾ lb
3 oz	Raw ham, cut into strips	75 g / 3 oz
¼ cup	Butter	50 g / 2 oz
1 lb	Ripe white grapes	500 g / 1 lb
Scant ¼ cup	Brandy	3 tbsp
½ cup	Coffee (single) cream	125 ml / 4 fl oz
2	Cloves	2
1 cup	Stock	225 ml / 8 fl oz
	Salt and pepper	
1	Sugar lump	1
½	Lemon	½

1. Lard the meat with small pieces of raw ham. Then tie the meat as for preparing a roast.
2. Melt the butter in a casserole, put in the piece of meat and brown it on all sides. Remove stones from grapes.
3. Blend grapes (or mash with a fork) together with brandy, sieve the mixture and pour the sauce over the meat. Add the cream, the cloves, ⅔ cup [150 ml / ¼ pint] stock, salt and pepper. Cover pan, lower heat and cook for 20 minutes.
4. Put a sugar lump in a small pan and caramelize it, dilute with the juice of half a lemon and a little hot stock, then pour over the meat. Continue cooking, still covered, for a further 10 minutes.
5. Remove the meat, slice it (remember to remove all the string) and place it onto a heated serving dish. Return the pan to the heat with the sauce, add butter and heat on a high flame so that it thickens; then pour it onto the meat. Garnish the edge of the dish with white grapes which can be fried in butter. Serve with sauté potatoes and a green salad.

Carpaccio alla toscana

Lemon Steak

🔪 01:00		00:00 🍳
American	**Ingredients**	**Metric/Imperial**
1 ¼ lb	Thin slices of fillet steak	600 g / 1 ¼ lb
3	Lemons	3
	Salt and pepper	
8	Small mushrooms (porcino)	8
2 oz	Grana cheese	50 g / 2 oz
2 tbsp	Chopped parsley	1 ½ tbsp

1. The meat must be sliced very thinly, as if it was ham; it is advisable to have the butcher cut it on a machine.
2. Arrange the thin slices of steak on a serving dish. Beat juice of lemons in a cup with salt and pepper and sprinkle the steak with the mixture.
3. After 30 minutes, when the meat has absorbed the dressing, slice the flesh of well cleaned raw mushrooms and lay them on top of the meat with some slices of grana cheese and chopped parsley. Serve immediately.

Scamone al forno 🧑‍🍳

Roast Silverside

🔪 00:10		00:30 🍳
	Cooling time 00:30 for joint	
American	**Ingredients**	**Metric/Imperial**
1 ¾ lb	Top round beef (silverside)	800 g / 1 ¾ lb
⅓ cup	Mustard	4 tbsp
2 tbsp	Vegetable oil	1 ½ tbsp
2 tbsp	Butter	25 g / 1 oz
	Salt and pepper	
2	Sprigs of rosemary	2
3 tbsp	White wine	2 tbsp
1 tbsp	Brandy	1 tbsp
⅓ cup	Fresh cream	4 tbsp

1. Preheat oven to 475°F / 240°C / Gas Mark 9.
2. Choose a good quality joint of silverside, remove excess fat and smear the joint well with all but 1 tablespoon of the mustard. Place in a roasting pan with oil, butter, salt, pepper and rosemary.
3. Roast in the oven allowing 15 minutes per 1 lb / 450 g for a rare joint and 20 minutes per 1 lb / 450 g for a well done joint, turning from time to time and moistening occasionally with white wine if the meat appears to be getting too dry.
4. Remove from oven, cool slightly in the pan, then transfer to a serving dish, cover with foil and cool completely at room temperature.
5. Discard rosemary, pour meat juices into a saucepan and heat through. Put remaining mustard into a cup, add brandy and cream, mix well and add to juices in pan mixing well, then pour into a jug. Serve the beef thinly sliced, with the sauce.

Bistecche arrotolate

Rolled Steaks

	00:10	00:10

American	Ingredients	Metric/Imperial
1 ¼ lb	Beef steak (fillet or rump)	600 g / 1 ¼ lb
4	Anchovies	4
16	Green olives	16
¼ cup	Butter	50 g / 2 oz
1 tbsp	Oil	1 tbsp
⅔ cup 3	Tomato sauce or canned tomatoes	150 ml / ¼ pint 3
½ tsp	Chopped oregano	½ tsp
	Salt and pepper	
1 tbsp	Capers	1 tbsp

1. Have the meat cut in approximately 6 in / 13 cm pieces and just over ¼ in / ½ cm thick.
2. Place an anchovy and 2 olives on each slice of meat. Fold the steak in half and close with a toothpick.
3. Heat butter and oil in a frying pan on a high heat and add the meat. Fry on both sides for 2 minutes, add the tomato sauce prepared in advance or the canned tomatoes crushed with a fork, oregano, pepper and salt, and cook slowly for 8 minutes.
4. Add chopped capers, cook for a further 2 minutes and serve hot.

Filetto estivo

Summer Steak

	00:30	00:15

American	Ingredients	Metric/Imperial
1 ¾ lb	Fillet steak	800 g / 1 ¾ lb
1 ¼ cups	Aspic	300 ml / ½ pint
2 tbsp	Vegetable oil	1 ½ tbsp
¼ cup	Butter	50 g / 2 oz
	Salt	

1. Brown a piece of fillet steak in oil and butter on a very high heat. When it browns on all sides, add salt, then lower the heat for a few minutes, keeping the pan covered, then switch off the heat.
2. Put the well drained fillet on a chopping board and slice it thinly; pour the cooking juices into a cup and place it in the coldest part of the refrigerator.
3. Make a jelly with the aspic and let it cool. Take the cup with meat juices from refrigerator, remove the fat which will have formed on the surface and pour the cooking juices in to the jelly. Pour a little of it over the meat which has been arranged on a plate and return to the refrigerator.
4. Serve the meat, decorated with the aspic cut into cubes.

BUYING AND COOKING PORK

American cuts to choose	Cooking methods
loin, crown, arm picnic shoulder, blade boston shoulder, tenderloin, back ribs, spareribs and country-style ribs	roast
rib chops, loin chops, shoulder steaks, cubes for kebabs, ground pork patties, sausages (fresh)	broil, fry
chops, spareribs and country-style ribs, back ribs, tenderloin, shoulder steaks, cubes	braise
spareribs and country-style ribs, hocks	stew

British cuts to choose	
fresh belly, leg, loin, neck end, spare rib, fillet, blade, hand, knuckle, spareribs	roast
chump chops, loin chops, spare rib chops, escalopes, cubes for kebabs, minced pork patties, sausages (fresh)	grill, fry
fillet, spare rib	braise
fresh belly, knuckle	stew

Lonza profumata

Pork in Brandy Sauce

🔪▭▷ 00:20   00:15 ▭◁

American	Ingredients	Metric/Imperial
1¾ lb	Loin of pork	800 g / 1¾ lb
8	Round slices of bacon	8
20	Sage leaves	20
½ tsp	Rosemary leaves, chopped	½ tsp
¼ cup	Butter	50 g / 2 oz
3 tbsp	Oil	2 tbsp
¼ cup	Brandy	50 ml / 2 fl oz
½	Stock cube	½

1. Cut the pork in thin slices, (about 2 per head) removing all excess fat. Lay a slice of bacon and two sage leaves on each piece of meat, roll up and secure with a toothpick.
2. Put the butter and oil into a wide pan and add remaining sage and the rosemary; as soon as the fat has heated, add the meat and pour on the brandy. Allow to cook for 10 minutes, moistening from time to time with boiling water in which a stock cube has been dissolved.
3. Strain the cooking juices into a sauceboat and serve with the meat and accompany with purée potatoes.

Filetto di maiale alle mele

Roast Pork with Apples

🔪▭▷ 00:15   00:40 ▭◁

American	Ingredients	Metric/Imperial
1 lb	Tender loin of pork (fillet)	500 g / 1 lb
Scant ¼ cup	Vegetable oil	3 tbsp
	Salt and pepper	
1¾ lb	Cooking apples	800 g / 1¾ lb
1 tbsp	Honey	1 tbsp
¾ cup	White wine	175 ml / 6 fl oz
½	Stock cube	½
2 tbsp	Butter	25 g / 1 oz

1. Preheat the oven to 350°F / 180°C / Gas Mark 4.
2. Trim the meat carefully and tie it with kitchen thread to keep it in shape. Lay it in a baking pan with oil, salt and pepper and cook in a moderate oven for about 30 minutes.
3. Peel and core the apples and slice them very thinly. Heat them for a few minutes in a separate pan with honey and white wine. Arrange the apples with their cooking syrup on a serving dish to make a bed for the roast pork.
4. After removing the string, slice the meat, arrange back together as though it were still whole.
5. Put the pan on the heat with the cooking juices from the meat, mixing them with boiling water mixed with half a stock cube. When the gravy has thickened a little, mix in a small piece of butter away from the heat. As soon as it has melted pour the hot sauce over the meat.

Polpettone al cognac

Meatloaf with Cognac

⊂▭══▷ 00:10   00:30 ⊂══▷

American	Ingredients	Metric/Imperial
1 lb	Ground (minced) pork	450 g / 1 lb
5 oz	Ricotta (curd cheese)	150 g / 5 oz
1	Egg	1
3 tbsp	Grated parmesan cheese	2 tbsp
	Salt and pepper	
¼ tsp	Nutmeg	¼ tsp
3 tbsp	Cognac	2 tbsp
3 tbsp	Oil	2 tbsp
1 tbsp	Butter	15 g / ½ oz

1. Mix all the ingredients (except the cognac, oil and butter) thoroughly, then press them firmly into one large round.
2. Sprinkle some of the cognac over the meatloaf, then heat the oil and butter and fry in a wide, heavy pan, add the meat, turn every now and then, taking great care that it does not stick to the bottom of the pan.
3. Continue to sprinkle with the cognac (the taste combines well with pork and ricotta). This meatloaf is a good choice for a picnic, but can be served hot.

Cosciotto di maiale alla grappa

Leg of Pork with Grappa

⊂▭══▷ 00:25   02:00 ⊂══▷

American	Ingredients	Metric/Imperial
1	Carrot	1
1	Celery stalk	1
1	Bay leaf	1
4	Sprigs of parsley	4
3	Garlic cloves	3
¼ cup	Vegetable oil	50 ml / 2 fl oz
2 tbsp	Butter	25 g / 1 oz
10 oz	Leeks	275 g / 10 oz
2 lb	Loin of pork (chine)	1 kg / 2 lb
½ cup	Vinegar	125 ml / 4 fl oz
½ cup	Dry white wine	125 ml / 4 fl oz
1	Stock cube	1
	Pepper	
¼ cup	Grappa	50 ml / 2 fl oz

1. Prepare a bouquet garni with carrot, celery, bay leaf and parsley tied together. Put the whole cloves of garlic in a large saucepan and fry them in the oil and the butter; add the vegetables which you have tied together, the leeks cut into rings and finally the meat. Brown and moisten with a little vinegar and then the dry white wine.
2. When the vegetables have softened and the wine has evaporated, add stock made with a cube and 2½ cups [600 ml / 1 pint] water and plenty of pepper.

3. Cover the pan and cook on a very low heat for about 2 hours, adding a little hot water from time to time whenever the sauce becomes too dry.
4. When the meat is quite tender, remove it from the heat and place it on one side. Strain the sauce and return it to the pan together with the meat. On a medium heat add the grappa; cook for another 10 minutes.
5. When the pork is cooked, cut it into thick slices and serve it with the sauce and an accompaniment of steamed potatoes or white rice.

Maiale alla bresciana

Pot-Roast of Pork with Artichoke Hearts

00:30   01:30

American	Ingredients	Metric/Imperial
1	Onion	1
1	Celery stalk	1
1	Carrot	1
¼ cup	Oil	50 ml / 2 fl oz
¼ cup	Butter	50 g / 2 oz
8	Artichoke hearts	8
¼ tsp	Chopped rosemary	¼ tsp
3 lb	Loin of pork, boned and rolled	1.4 kg / 3 lb
1 cup	Red wine	225 ml / 8 fl oz
	Salt and pepper	
14 oz	Small potatoes	400 g / 14 oz
1	Stock cube	1
Sauce (optional)		
2 tbsp	Mustard	1½ tbsp
1	Egg yolk	1
4	Anchovy fillets	4
1 cup	Coffee (single) cream	225 ml / 8 fl oz

1. Chop the onion, celery and carrot and fry lightly in oil and butter. Add the artichoke hearts and a little rosemary. Remove and set the vegetables aside on a plate, put the meat into the pan; brown quickly over a high heat, turning constantly.
2. Pour some red wine over the meat and allow to evaporate, season with salt and pepper. Now tip the vegetables into the pan with the meat and add the peeled potatoes; reduce the heat and add some stock made with the stock cube dissolved in boiling water.
3. Cook for about 1 hour, adding a small quantity of wine from time to time.
4. When the meat is cooked, cut it into thick slices and place on a heated serving dish. Arrange the potatoes around it and sieve or blend the vegetables and remaining liquid which can either be served separately or poured over the meat.
5. Serve with mustard or, if preferred, with a sauce made from mustard, egg yolk, a few chopped anchovy fillets and single cream beaten together.

Spiedini in padella

Fried Kebabs

	00:20	00:20

American	Ingredients	Metric/Imperial
11 oz	Pork fillet	300 g / 11 oz
7 oz	Italian sausage	200 g / 7 oz
7 oz	Liver	200 g / 7 oz
1	Onion	1
1	Sweet pepper	1
	Sage leaves, as required	
1 tsp	Chopped rosemary	1 tsp
1 tbsp	Vegetable oil	1 tbsp
1 tbsp	Butter	1 tbsp
1 quart	Stock (cubes dissolved in hot water)	1 litre / 1¾ pints
1 tbsp	Brandy	1 tbsp
	Salt and pepper	

1. Cut up all the meat into fair-sized chunks, peel and slice onion and deseed and slice sweet pepper.
2. Thread meat and vegetables onto prepared skewers, alternating the varieties, e.g. pork fillet, sausage, liver and sage, finishing with a slice of onion and one of sweet pepper.
3. Heat oil and butter in a large frying pan and brown skewers all over. Add stock and cook a further 10 minutes. Season with salt and pepper, increase heat and pour over brandy.
4. Remove skewers and put in a deep serving dish. Pour over some sauce and serve remaining sauce separately.

Mini-pig allo spiedo

Spit-Roasted Suckling-Pig

	00:30	02:30

American	Ingredients	Metric/Imperial
1	Suckling-pig (small, lean piglet)	1
1 cup	Oil	225 ml / 8 fl oz
	Salt and pepper	
2	Onions	2
½ cup	Cognac	125 ml / 4 fl oz
1	Garlic clove	1
3	Bay leaves	3

1. Choose a very small piglet, weighing no more than 22 lb [10 kg]. Season the inside with oil, salt and pepper, rub with onions and pour in the cognac. Using strong kitchen string, tie the feet close to the body. Rub oil over the entire skin surface then impale the piglet on the spit.
2. Put oil, salt and pepper into a cup and beat well; add a crushed clove of garlic and some crumbled bay leaves.
3. Start roasting over a good heat. The small piglet will take at least 2 hours to roast and it must be continually brushed with the oil mixture.

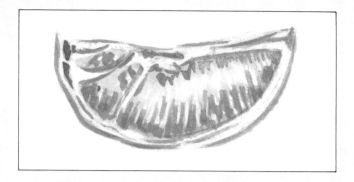

Arrosto di maiale all'arancia

Roast Pork with Orange

	00:35		02:10	
	Serves 6			

American	Ingredients	Metric/Imperial
1	Onion	1
1	Garlic clove	1
½ cup	Vegetable oil	125 ml / 4 fl oz
1 tsp	Lard	1 tsp
1	Sweet red pepper	1
4-6	Oranges	4-6
	Salt	
1 tsp	Sugar	1 tsp
4 lb	Boned leg of pork	2 kg / 4 lb
½ tsp	Powdered thyme	½ tsp
½ tsp	Chopped rosemary	½ tsp
½ tsp	Chopped mint	½ tsp
¼ tsp	Cayenne pepper	¼ tsp
1 ⅓ cups	Rice	250 g / 9 oz
⅓ cup	Olives	50 g / 2 oz
3 tbsp	Rum	2 tbsp

1. Preheat the oven to 350°F / 180°C / Gas Mark 4. Prepare the sauce, which will be used to moisten the roast.
2. Finely chop the onion and garlic and put in half the heated oil and the lard to brown for 4 minutes. Add the deseeded, chopped red sweet pepper, the grated peel of 2 oranges and the juice of 4 ripe oranges. Season with a little salt and sugar.
3. Rub the pork with a mixture of salt, remaining oil, powdered thyme, chopped fresh rosemary, chopped mint and a little cayenne pepper. Place the spiced meat on an oiled rack in a preheated oven.
4. During cooking brush the meat frequently with the sauce. If it becomes too thick add a little more orange juice. Cook for about 2 hours.
5. Cook rice until 'al dente', drain and keep warm in the oven.
6. When the roast is well cooked, remove from the oven and leave for 10 minutes, then cut into slices about ¼ in / 5 mm in thickness and arrange them on a serving dish. Garnish with slices of 2 oranges and olives and cover with the sauce, diluted with a little orange juice and a little rum. Serve surrounded by boiled rice.

Carré di maiale alla boema

Loin of Pork Bohemian-Style

	00:30		01:30

American	Ingredients	Metric/Imperial
2 lb	Onions	1 kg / 2 lb
2 lb	Pork loin (chine)	1 kg / 2 lb
2 tbsp	Vegetable oil	25 ml / 1 fl oz
3 tbsp	Butter	40 g / 1½ oz
1 quart	Light beer	1 litre / 1¾ pints
¼ cup	Flour	25 g / 1 oz
6	Fennel seeds	6
¼ cup	Coffee (single) cream	50 ml / 2 fl oz
3 tbsp	Gin	2 tbsp

1. Put the onions, peeled and cut into slices, into a bowl and add sufficient cold water to cover and allow to rest for about 30 minutes.

2. Fry the pork in a large pan with the oil and 2 tablespoons [25 g / 1 oz] butter until it is browned on all sides. Add the drained onions to the pan with the pork and sweat them very gently for about 10 minutes.

3. Remove the pan from the heat and pour in the beer in a thin stream to cover the meat; return to the heat and bring to the boil. Cook uncovered on a medium high heat until the beer has completely evaporated, taking care not to let the meat stick to the bottom of the pan.

4. When the meat is tender, remove it from the heat and put it on a plate; strain the cooking liquid and put it in a separate pan with remainder of butter, flour, a few fennel seeds, cream and the gin.

5. Return the meat to the pan and continue cooking over a gentle heat for 10 minutes.

6. Cut the meat into slices, place them on a serving dish and cover with the sauce.

7. Serve accompanied with boiled vegetables garnished with parsley and glasses of beer.

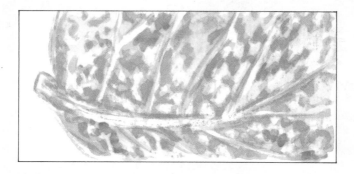

Cassoeula o posciandra o bottaggio

Pork and Sausage Casserole

American	Ingredients	Metric/Imperial
1	Onion	1
1	Large slice of fat bacon	1
2 tbsp	Vegetable oil	25 ml / 1 fl oz
2 tbsp	Butter	25 g / 1 oz
1	Carrot	1
1	Celery stalk	1
1 lb	Pork ribs	500 g / 1 lb
1	Pig's head (snout and ear)	1
7 oz	Pork rind	200 g / 7 oz
1 tbsp	Tomato purée	1 tbsp
1	Stock cube	1
	Salt and pepper	
2	Savoy cabbages	2
7 oz	Thin budello sausage	200 g / 7 oz
½ tsp	Spices (optional)	½ tsp

1. Chop the onion finely and brown it with chopped fat bacon or with oil and butter.

2. When the ingredients have softened, add the carrot and celery, also chopped very finely, and cook on a gentle heat, moistening with water if it is really necessary.

3. Boil separately the ribs, snout and rind until tender then cut into large pieces. Retain stock.

4. When the vegetables have softened, add the ribs, the snout and the rind, add the tomato purée diluted with a little warm water, pour in 2½ cups [1 pint / 600 ml] of stock made with the cube and cook through on a low flame, covered.

5. Preheat the oven to 325°F / 160°C / Gas Mark 3.

6. Strip the leaves from the cabbages, eliminating the tougher parts, rinse the leaves under running water, shred coarsely and mix with the meat, a little at a time. Season with salt and pepper and spices.

7. Cut the sausage into pieces, put it into a baking pan adding a drop of water and place it in the oven, covered and at a low heat. When the fat has melted, add the sausage to the casserole, cook for 1 hour in the oven. Serve piping hot with crusty bread.

Costine con i crauti

Pork Ribs with Cabbage

| | 00:40 | | 02:15 | |

American	Ingredients	Metric/Imperial
3 ¼ lb	Pork spare ribs	1.5 kg / 3 ¼ lb
¼ cup	Butter	50 g / 2 oz
½ cup	Dry white wine	225 ml / 8 fl oz
	Salt and pepper	
1	Stock cube	1
1	Large cabbage	1
1	Onion	1
2 oz	Smoked bacon	50 g / 2 oz
¼ cup	Vinegar	50 ml / 2 fl oz

1. Cut the pork ribs into pieces and brown them in a little butter, then drain off the fat and place them in another pan.
2. Moisten with dry white wine, and when it has evaporated, season with salt and pepper. Add 2½ cups [600 ml / 1 pint] stock made from the cube and cook slowly for 2 hours.
3. Cut a firm cabbage into thin strips, wash and place in a pan, pour over 2½ cups [600 ml / 1 pint] boiling water and cook for 10 minutes.
4. Gently cook the chopped onion in a very large saucepan with a little butter and the chopped smoked bacon, add the well drained cabbage, season with salt and pepper and cook covered for about 30 minutes, adding stock from time to time.
5. After 20 minutes add the vinegar and allow to evaporate over a brisk heat.
6. Add the cabbage to the pork ribs and let them cook together for a further 15 minutes. Serve very hot with mustard.

Maialetto di Paolo

Cold Loin of Pork with Tuna Sauce

| | 00:20 | | 01:00 | |

American	Ingredients	Metric/Imperial
2 lb	Loin of pork without bones or fat	1 kg / 2 lb
9 oz	Tuna in oil	250 g / 9 oz
1	Onion	1
4	Anchovies	4
	Salt and pepper	
2 cups	White wine	450 ml / ¾ pint
2 tsp	Cognac	2 tsp
¼ cup	Vegetable oil	50 ml / 2 fl oz
2	Lemons	2

1. Bone the loin of pork or buy one boned and discard all the fat. (The bones may be used next day for stock and pork fat is always useful for frying.)

2. Put the meat into a large saucepan with the chopped tuna, the thinly sliced onion, the washed, boned and broken up anchovies, salt, pepper, white wine and cognac. Cover and cook over moderate heat. Test the pork by inserting a toothpick, when it enters easily, the meat is cooked.

3. Transfer the pork, sliced, to a large serving dish and tip the remaining contents of the saucepan into a large bowl, mix oil and lemon juice and pour over the meat. Decorate with chopped gherkins.

Cook's tip: This dish must be prepared at least 12 hours in advance to allow the pork to absorb the flavor of the sauce. It will keep well in the refrigerator for several days.

Rostiscianna con polenta

Mixed Meat Stew with Polenta

01:00   01:30

American	Ingredients	Metric/Imperial
½ lb	Pork	225 g / 8 oz
½ lb	Beef	225 g / 8 oz
½ lb	Italian sausage	225 g / 8 oz
½ lb	Pork spare rib	225 g / 8 oz
¼ cup	Butter	50 g / 2 oz
¼ cup	Oil	50 ml / 2 fl oz
2 or 3	Onions	2 or 3
1	Carrot	1
1	Celery stalk	1
1½ cups	Dry red wine (Barbera)	350 ml / 12 fl oz
14 oz	Peeled tomatoes	400 g / 14 oz
2 lb	Red onions	1 kg / 2 lb
	Salt	
¾ lb	Coarse-grained corn meal for polenta	350 g / 12 oz

1. Cut all the meat into pieces of roughly equal size and place in a saucepan with heated butter, oil and 2 or 3 chopped onions. Add the chopped carrot and celery.

2. Stir and brown slightly then add the wine and, when it has been absorbed, the tomatoes.

3. Stir then add the chopped onions, and cook with the lid on for 20 minutes. Stir again and leave to simmer covered, until the meat is done.

4. Prepare the polenta by bringing 1½ quarts [1.5 litres / 2½ pints] of salted water to the boil and then adding the corn meal in a slow, steady, thin trickle, stirring constantly with a wooden spoon. Continue to stir for the full 20 minutes the polenta takes to cook. Add a little oil at the last moment.

5. Warm a large, deep serving dish. To serve, turn out the polenta onto the warmed dish, make a hollow in the centre and fill this with the piping hot meat stew.

Carré della Maremma

Loin of Pork 'Maremma'

| | 00:30 | | 01:30 | |

American	Ingredients	Metric/Imperial
2 lb	Loin of pork, boned	1 kg / 2 lb
¼ lb	Fat bacon	100 g / 4 oz
	Salt and pepper	
3 or 4	Cloves	3 or 4
¼ cup	Vegetable oil	50 ml / 2 fl oz
6	Sage leaves	6
3	Sprigs of rosemary	3
½	Onion	½
1	Celery stalk	1
1 tbsp	Chopped parsley	1 tbsp
¼ cup	Butter	50 g / 2 oz
½ cup	Red wine	125 ml / 4 fl oz
1	Stock cube	1
1	Garlic clove	1
¼ lb	Canadian (lean) bacon	100 g / 4 oz
1 lb	Plum tomatoes	500 g / 1 lb
2 lb	Swiss chard	1 kg / 2 lb

1. Have the butcher bone the pork for you, stick in pieces of fat bacon dipped in salt and pepper and a few cloves. Paint with oil, coat with coarse salt, sage and rosemary. Tie it tightly with white thread.

2. Chop the onion with a little celery and parsley. Heat oil and butter, cook vegetables gently on a low heat in a large casserole, adding the meat. Moisten with dry full-bodied red wine. Allow the wine to evaporate, add some stock made from the cube and continue cooking, adding more stock from time to time.

3. Fry crushed cloves of garlic in a small pan with a little oil, add a little finely chopped bacon and some chopped, peeled, tomatoes with the seeds removed; pour in a little hot water and cook very gently until a reduced sauce has formed.

4. Separately boil some Swiss chard, using only the white part. When cooked, drain and mix the chard with the tomato sauce, seasoning well.

5. Cut the meat into slices and arrange it on a heated dish covered with the cooking sauce and with the chard around it.

Arista di maiale alla panna

Pork Ribs with Cream

| | 00:25 | | 01:15 | |

American	Ingredients	Metric/Imperial
3¼ lb	Pork shoulder butt (chine)	1.5 kg / 3¼ lb
4	Garlic cloves	4
10	Cloves	10
½ cup	Vegetable oil	125 ml / 4 fl oz
3 or 4	Sprigs of rosemary	3 or 4
1 cup	Whipping (double) cream	225 ml / 8 fl oz
½ cup	Cognac, rum or grappa	125 ml / 4 fl oz
	Salt and pepper	

1. Preheat oven to 400°F / 200°C / Gas Mark 6.
2. Insert into the meat the cloves of garlic (cut in pieces) and alternate with the cloves; brush with oil. Tie a few sprigs of rosemary to the meat with thin white thread. Put the pork in an ovenproof dish, pour oil over it and put in the oven.
3. After 10 minutes cooking, turn the meat and roast it well on all sides.
4. Beat cream in a bowl with a glass of spirits (cognac, rum or grappa according to your own preference).
5. When the pork has been cooking for 30 minutes, lower the oven to 325°F / 170°C / Gas Mark 4 and moisten with the cream and liquor, pouring it all over the meat at once. Continue cooking for a further 30 minutes, taking care that the cooking juices do not dry out too much and turning the meat from time to time. If the sauce reduces too much, add a very little warm water.
6. Test the sauce and season with salt and pepper to taste. Remove the meat from the pan, strain sauce, slice the meat, cover it with the sauce and place the serving dish in the oven for a few moments before serving very hot.

Spiedini di fegato nella rete

Liver Kebabs in Caul

| | 00:40 | | 00:15 | |

American	Ingredients	Metric/Imperial
1	Piece of caul	1
1 lb	Pig's liver	½ kg / 1 lb
	Slices of bread	
8	Bay leaves	8
	Oil	
	Salt and pepper	
8	Lemon slices	8
	Parsley	

1. Soften caul fat in tepid water for 30 minutes then drain.
2. Cut liver into thick slices and wrap each piece in caul fat.
3. Thread skewers with slices or bread, liver and bay leaves. Brush with oil, season and place under a medium broiler (grill). Cook for 10-15 minutes, turning skewers from time to time.
4. Put skewers on a hot serving dish and garnish with lemon slices and parsley sprigs.

Italian Meat Dishes

Maiale alla ciociara

Pork Pasties

American	Ingredients	Metric/Imperial
3 tbsp	Oil	2 tbsp
¾ lb	Ground (minced) pork	350 g / 12 oz
2	Eggs	2
2	Italian sausages	2
1 cup	Grated parmesan cheese	100 g / 4 oz
2	Potatoes, boiled and mashed	2
¼ tsp	Nutmeg	¼ tsp
4	Sage leaves	4
½ lb	Short crust pastry	225 g / 8 oz
½ cup	Butter	100 g / 4 oz

00:30   **00:40**

1. Preheat the oven to 400°F / 200°C / Gas Mark 6.
2. Heat the oil in a pan and cook the pork for 8 minutes, drain on to a plate and allow to cool.
3. Put the ground (minced) pork, eggs, sausages, (skinned and chopped), parmesan and potatoes into a bowl and mix thoroughly. Add a little grated nutmeg and a few chopped sage leaves.
4. Divide the pastry into 4 portions. Roll each into a round. Divide the pork mixture into 4 and heap onto each pastry round. Damp and seal the edges.
5. Grease a baking tray, lay the pasties on the tray and bake in a hot oven for 15 minutes. Reduce the oven temperature to 325°F / 170°C / Gas Mark 3 and cook for a further 15 minutes.

Spezzatino tirolese

Tyrolean Stew

00:30 Marinating time 01:00   **01:30**

American	Ingredients	Metric/Imperial
2 lb	Pork loin	1 kg / 2 lb
1 cup	Red wine	225 ml / 8 fl oz
Scant ¼ cup	Vegetable oil	3 tbsp
	Salt and pepper	
3	Cloves	3
2	Bay leaves	2
2 oz	Bacon	50 g / 2 oz
1	Onion	1
1 tbsp	Butter	15 g / ½ oz
11 oz	Italian sausage	300 g / 11 oz
8 oz	Peeled tomatoes	225 g / 8 oz
3	Potatoes	3
½	Stock cube	½

1. Trim fat and cut the pork into small pieces, marinate in an earthenware pot with the red wine, oil, salt, pepper, cloves, and bay leaves. Cover and leave at room temperature for 1 hour.

2. Chop the bacon and onion very finely and fry gently in a little butter and oil for 4 minutes, then add the sausage cut into small pieces and fry it so that the fat melts a little.

3. Add the marinated meat and fry it over a high heat, stir in the marinating juices with the cloves and bay leaves and evaporate. Moisten with 2 cups [450 ml / ¾ pint] of hot water and add the tomatoes.

4. Cover and cook on a moderate heat for about 45 minutes.

5. Add the peeled potatoes, cut into small pieces, check the seasoning and if necessary add either half a stock cube or a little salt, or both. Cook for a further 50 minutes.

6. Accompany this dish with polenta or with thick slices of crusty brown bread.

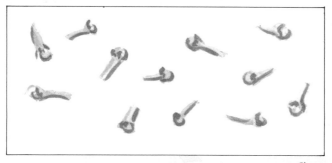

Cloves

Fegato e peperoni alla russa

Liver and Peppers

00:40
Soaking time 02:00

00:30

American	Ingredients	Metric/Imperial
1 lb	Pigs' liver	500 g / 1 lb
⅔ cup	Milk	150 ml / ¼ pint
1 cup	Vegetable oil	225 ml / 8 fl oz
¼ cup	Butter	50 g / 2 oz
	Salt and pepper	
3 tbsp	Red wine vinegar	2 tbsp
2	Onions	2
3	Sweet peppers	3
5	Ripe tomatoes (fresh or canned)	5
1 tsp	Cayenne pepper	1 tsp
7 oz	Stale bread cut into cubes	200 g / 7 oz

1. Soak the pigs' liver in milk for 2 hours. Drain and dry with kitchen towels. Cook slices of liver in a pan with quarter of the oil and the butter. Season with salt and pepper, add red wine vinegar and let it evaporate. As soon as the liver is cooked, remove it from the pan and place it on a plate.

2. Heat remaining butter and some oil. Fry the onions in a high-sided pan.

3. Remove the seeds and pith from the peppers, cut into strips, add to the onions with the chopped tomatoes and cook over a brisk heat. Season with salt, pepper and plenty of cayenne pepper.

4. Add the liver and mix thoroughly with the sauce.

5. Fry the cubes of stale bread separately in the remaining heated oil, drain and serve round the liver.

BUYING AND COOKING LAMB

American cuts to choose	Cooking methods
leg, crown roast, rack or rib, shoulder	roast
shoulder chops, rib chops, loin chops, sirloin chops, leg chops or steaks, cubes for kebabs, ground lamb patties	broil, fry
neck slices, shoulder chops, breast, riblets, shanks, lamb for stew	braise, stew
British cuts to choose	
best end of neck, breast, leg (including fillet and knuckle), loin, saddle, shoulder	roast
chump chops, cutlets, loin chops, lamb steaks from the leg, noisettes (boneless loin or best end steaks), cubes for kebabs, minced lamb patties	grill, fry
shoulder, middle neck cutlets, breast, chump chops, loin chops, leg	braise
middle neck, scrag end of neck	stew

Montone all'abruzzese
Casserole of Mutton with Wine and Herbs

| | 00:20 | | 02:10 | |

American	Ingredients	Metric/Imperial
2 lb	Mutton (shoulder or neck)	1 kg / 2 lb
Scant ¼ cup	Oil	3 tbsp
4	Bay leaves	4
½ tsp	Chopped basil	½ tsp
½ tsp	Chopped rosemary	½ tsp
2	Garlic cloves	2
	Salt and pepper	
½	Chilli pepper	½
2 cups	Dry white wine	450 ml / ¾ pint

1. Dice the meat, heat the oil in a saucepan or casserole over a medium heat, add meat, turning until brown.
2. Chop the bay leaves, basil and rosemary, sprinkle over the meat, which should be stirred frequently.
3. Add crushed garlic, salt, several twists of pepper, a piece of chilli, the wine, and 1 cup [225 ml / 8 fl oz] water, cover and cook gently for 2 hours either on top of the stove or in a medium oven.

Umido alla pugliese
Lamb Stew with Pasta

| | 00:15 | | 01:30 | |

American	Ingredients	Metric/Imperial
1¾ lb	Stewing lamb	800 g / 1¾ lb
2	Onions	2
1¼ lb	Tomatoes	600 g / 1¼ lb
3 tbsp	Vegetable oil	2 tbsp
1 tbsp	White flour	1 tbsp
⅔ cup	Red wine	150 ml / 5 fl oz
2	Lemons	2
1 lb	Orecchiette or other pasta	450 g / 1 lb
	Sprigs of parsley	
	Salt and pepper	

1. Dice meat, peel and chop onions, peel tomatoes. Heat oil and sauté meat and onions for 3-4 minutes until meat is brown.
2. Add flour to pan then cook for 1 minute. Remove from the heat and pour over wine, lemon juice and stir in tomatoes. Return to heat, cover and simmer for about 1¼ hours, stirring from time to time.
3. Meanwhile cook pasta in plenty of boiling salted water until 'al dente'. Stir cooked pasta into stew.
4. Spoon stew into an earthenware dish, garnish with sprigs of parsley, add a sprinkling of black pepper and serve.

Abbacchio aglio e aceto

Lamb with Garlic and Vinegar

| | 00:30 | 01:30 |

American	Ingredients	Metric/Imperial
2 lb	Lamb (neck, shoulder, breast)	1 kg / 2 lb
¼ cup	Vegetable oil	50 ml / 2 fl oz
6	Garlic cloves	6
6	Sprigs of rosemary	6
	Salt and pepper	
2	Boned anchovies	2
½ cup	Vinegar	125 ml / 4 fl oz

1. Preheat the oven to 350°F / 180°C / Gas Mark 4.
2. Wash and thoroughly dry the meat, cut in pieces, then put in an ovenproof dish to brown with oil, 2 crushed cloves of garlic and rosemary in the oven for 15 minutes, turning from time to time. Season with pepper and a very little salt.
3. Crush the anchovies in a mortar or blender with 4 cloves of garlic, dilute the pulp with red or white vinegar, according to taste, to obtain a generous quantity of sauce.
4. When the lamb is well browned on all sides, pour over the sauce with 1 cup [225 ml / 8 fl oz] water and continue cooking on a medium heat on the stove or in the oven, as you wish.
5. Remove the meat from the pan to a heated serving dish. Dilute the sauce with a little water if it has reduced too much, pour into a sauceboat and serve separately with the lamb.

Scottadito

Lamb Chops Fried in Pecorino Batter

| | 00:30 | 00:10 |

American	Ingredients	Metric/Imperial
1	Rack (best end neck) of young spring lamb	1
2	Eggs	2
¼ cup	Grated pecorino (sheep's milk cheese)	25 g / 1 oz
	Salt and pepper	
1 tbsp	Chopped parsley	1 tbsp
½ cup	Very fine bread crumbs	50 g / 2 oz
2	Garlic cloves	2
2 tbsp	Vegetable oil	2 tbsp
6	Lemon slices	6

1. Ask the butcher to remove the corner bone and backbone, leaving just the rib. Using a very sharp knife, lay bone bare up to the level of the fillet (but not cutting through the meat). Take this strip of meat, wrap it around the fillet and secure with a cocktail stick. Flatten into a cutlet shape.

2. Preheat oven to 300°F / 150°C / Gas Mark 2.

3. Prepare batter by beating eggs and adding grated pecorino, chopped parsley, salt and pepper. Dip cutlets in this mixture and then coat with bread crumbs.

4. Cut cloves of garlic in half, heat oil in the frying pan and sauté garlic for 1 minute, then remove. Add cutlets to the pan and fry, browning well on both sides. Remove with a slotted spoon and drain on absorbent kitchen towels. Put on a serving dish and keep warm in the oven.

5. Cut 6 strips of kitchen foil, about 2 × 2¾ in / 5 × 7 cm, fringe and wrap around exposed bones of cutlets.

6. Serve cutlets garnished with lemon slices accompanied with artichoke hearts fried in bread crumbs.

Abbacchio e carciofi

Lamb with Artichokes

01:00   01:00

American	Ingredients	Metric/Imperial
2	Whole lamb loins	2
¼ cup	Butter	50 g / 2 oz
¼ cup	Vegetable oil	50 ml / 2 fl oz
6	Sage leaves	6
6	Sprigs of rosemary	6
	Salt and pepper	
1 cup	Dry white wine	225 ml / 8 fl oz
8	Small artichokes	8
2	Eggs	2
1 cup	Bread crumbs	100 g / 4 oz
½	Lemon	½
	Oil for deep frying	

1. Preheat the oven to 400°F / 200°C / Gas Mark 6.

2. Wash and thoroughly dry the lamb. Heat the butter and oil in a roasting pan, adding a few sage leaves, rosemary and seasoning with salt and pepper. Put the lamb in the pan and brown on all sides in the oven.

3. Moisten the lamb with the white wine, adding a little at a time so that one amount is absorbed before adding another.

4. While the lamb is cooking, clean the artichokes, remove the tough leaves, chokes and thorns, and boil them for 10 minutes or so. Remove them from the heat and drain upside down on a wire rack to extract all the water.

5. Cut the artichokes in two, dry them well, then coat them with the beaten eggs and the bread crumbs. Fry them on a brisk heat in plenty of oil.

6. Squeeze a few drops of lemon juice onto the artichokes, when cooked, then remove them from the pan and put to dry on a sheet of kitchen towel which will soak up the excess grease; then sprinkle with grated lemon rind.

7. Finish cooking the lamb; there should be no juices left at the end of cooking. Place in the centre of a heated serving dish and surround with the fried artichokes.

Agnello al limone 👨‍🍳

Lamb with Lemon

	00:30	01:00
	Marinating time 02:00	
	Serves 6	

American	Ingredients	Metric/Imperial
3 lb	Leg of lamb	1.4 kg / 3 lb
2	Garlic cloves	2
2	Lemons	2
	Salt and pepper	
¾ cup	Vegetable oil	175 ml / 6 fl oz
½ tsp	Chopped sage	½ tsp
½ tsp	Chopped rosemary	½ tsp
2½ cups	White wine	600 ml / 1 pint
½ cup	Wine vinegar	125 ml / 4 fl oz
14 oz	Plum tomatoes, fresh or canned	400 g / 14 oz
1 cup	Black olives	175 g / 6 oz
	New potatoes	

1. Cut meat into 1 in / 2½ cm cubes, mix with the crushed garlic and lemon juice and pour over the lamb with salt and pepper. Marinate for 2 hours.
2. Heat the oil in a large frying pan, add the chopped sage and rosemary. When the fat is hot, brown the pieces of lamb well on all sides. Moisten a little at a time with the white wine mixed with the vinegar, then cover with the tomatoes, which can be broken down with a wooden spoon, and add the black olives.
3. Cook over a low heat, or continue cooking in the oven at 325°F / 170°C / Gas Mark 3.
4. Remove the meat from the pan when it is well cooked with a slotted spoon. Sieve the sauce, if necessary thickening it with a little flour or thinning with a little wine. Reheat and serve very hot, surrounded by boiled new potatoes.

Costolette di agnello con patate al vino 👨‍🍳

Lamb Cutlets with Potatoes in Wine

	00:40	00:20
	Serves 6	

American	Ingredients	Metric/Imperial
12	Lamb cutlets	12
¼ cup	Flour	25 g / 1 oz
½ cup	Butter	100 g / 4 oz
4	Garlic cloves	4
4	Sage leaves	4
½ cup	Dry white wine	125 ml / 4 fl oz
2 lb	Potatoes	1 kg / 2 lb
¾ cup	Olive oil	175 ml / 6 fl oz
2	Onions	2
	Salt	
½ tsp	Hot paprika	½ tsp

1. Coat the cutlets in flour, heat the butter in a pan and fry until golden brown for about 3 minutes each side.

2. Add the crushed garlic and sage, pour in the wine and cook on a low heat for 10 minutes.

3. Peel the potatoes and cut into thick slices (alternatively if they are small to medium-sized, cut into quarters), cook in boiling salted water until tender but firm.

4. Heat the oil in a pan over a medium heat and cook the thinly sliced onions for 4 minutes.

5. Add the potatoes to the onion and fry, turning from time to time, without breaking the potatoes too much. Sprinkle with salt and paprika.

6. Serve the cooked cutlets on a heated serving dish garnished with potatoes and onions.

Montone al pilaff

Mutton Pilaff

00:20   01:00

American	Ingredients	Metric/Imperial
⅔ cup	Oil	150 ml / ¼ pint
2	Garlic cloves	2
1 ¼ lb	Stewing mutton	600 g / 1 ¼ lb
3	Onions	3
1 ½ cups	Rice	350 g / 12 oz
10	Strands of saffron	10
3 tbsp	Rosewater	2 tbsp
	Salt and pepper	
1 tsp	Sugar	1 tsp
1 quart	Stock	1 litre / 1 ¾ pints
¼ cup	Raisins	40 g / 1 ½ oz
1 tsp	Chopped mint	1 tsp
1 tsp	Chopped sage	1 tsp
1 ½ oz	Pine kernels	40 g / 1 ½ oz

1. Choose a large pan with a lid. Heat the oil and fry the garlic cloves, remove when brown.

2. Cut the mutton into small dice and put in the oil, cook for about 10 minutes until brown. Add roughly chopped onions, the washed and drained rice. When the rice has become transparent, add the saffron, dissolved in rosewater, the salt, pepper, sugar and stock. Stir well and cover.

3. When the rice has absorbed all the liquid, test the meat then add the raisins, chopped mint and sage. Remove the pan from the stove and allow it to stand for a few minutes in a warm place. Pile pilaff onto a heated serving dish and garnish with lightly toasted pine kernels. This dish must be served piping hot.

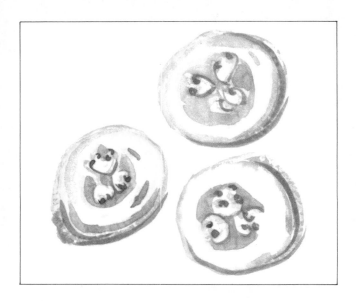

Frittura mista

Fried Mixed Grill

	00:40		00:20

American	Ingredients	Metric/Imperial
1 ¼ cups	Flour	150 g / 5 oz
3 tbsp	Olive oil	2 tbsp
2	Eggs	2
	Salt and pepper	
3 tbsp	Dry white wine	2 tbsp
3	Artichokes	3
½	Lemon	½
5 oz	Calf's brains	150 g / 5 oz
5 oz	Calf's liver	150 g / 5 oz
¾ lb	Zucchini (courgettes)	350 g / 12 oz
4	Lamb chops	4
½ tsp	Curry powder	½ tsp
1 ¼ cups	Vegetable oil for frying	300 ml / ½ pint
1	Bay leaf	1
1	Sage leaf	1

1. Prepare the batter, putting the flour in a large bowl, add olive oil, the egg yolks and a pinch of salt. Mix carefully and add the white wine and sufficient water so that the batter is not too thick.

2. Clean the artichokes and cook them for 5 minutes in water with a little lemon juice. Immerse the carefully cleaned calf's brains and liver in boiling water; steep for 5 minutes.

3. Cut all the meat and vegetables into thin slices or small pieces. Whip the egg whites until they are stiff and fold them gently into the batter, taking care that they do not collapse, add a little curry powder, tip in the meat and vegetables and mix so that they are all well covered.

4. Heat the oil in a large deep frying pan with a bay leaf and a leaf of sage and put the ingredients into the pan in batches and fry until golden brown. Drain on absorbent kitchen towels.

Rognoni alla senape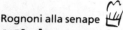

Kidneys in Mustard Sauce

	00:20		00:00

American	Ingredients	Metric/Imperial
8	Lambs' kidneys	8
¼ cup	Butter	50 g / 2 oz
2	Garlic cloves	2
1 cup	Dry white wine	225 ml / 8 fl oz
1 tbsp	Mustard	1 tbsp
4 drops	Worcester sauce	4 drops
Scant ¼ cup	Chopped parsley	3 tbsp

1. Skin and core the kidneys, scald in boiling water for a few minutes and drain. Slice or halve the kidneys.
2. Heat the butter in a heavy pan with the garlic, add kidneys and fry over a medium heat for 5 minutes, then add the white wine and turn the heat up to allow it to evaporate.
3. Reduce the heat to moderate and continue cooking for another 10 minutes, add the mustard and a few drops of Worcester sauce. Stir well, sprinkle with parsley and serve hot with a purée of potatoes.

Montone del capraio

Mutton with Bread and Onions

Traditionally, this dish was cooked in a low-burning wood-fired range using a copper pan with a very tight-fitting lid. Nowadays the pressure cooker makes an ideal substitute.

	00:10		00:30 in a pressure cooker

American	Ingredients	Metric/Imperial
¼ cup	Butter	50 g / 2 oz
1	Onion	1
2 lb	Stewing mutton	1 kg / 2 lb
	Salt and pepper	
8	Slices of crusty bread	8

1. Melt the butter in the pressure cooker, fry the chopped onion. Cut the meat into small pieces, add to the onion, season with salt and pepper. Pour over 1 cup [225 ml / 8 fl oz] water, close the cooker lid, bring to pressure and cook for 20 minutes over moderate heat.
2. De-pressurize the cooker, remove the meat and serve on thick slices of toast with all the juices poured over it.

POULTRY

Choosing and keeping poultry
The drumsticks should be plump and the breastbone soft and pliable. The skin should be smooth and glossy. Soft flesh tinged with red should be avoided. Ask your supplier for advice and look at the sell-by date on pre-wrapped poultry.

Cooked poultry will keep in the refrigerator for 3-4 days. In a sauce, it will not keep for more than two days. Uncooked poultry, which is not to be frozen, should be consumed quickly – within two days. After buying, remove the wrapping, cover the bird with wax [greaseproof] paper and refrigerate.

To barbecue chicken
Chicken, turkey and duck are all suitable for cooking on a barbecue. Whole chicken and duck can be spit roasted, turkey is more suitable cut into portions.

A whole bird, about 4 lb / 2 kg, will need about 2 hours over a good fire. Portions will take anything from 25 to 30 minutes for drumsticks, to 1 hour for large pieces.

All poultry will have a better flavor if marinated for several hours before cooking. Baste the poultry meat with either melted butter or oil during cooking but only baste with marinade toward the end of the cooking time.

Red wine marinade
Mix 1¼ cups [150 ml / ¼ pint] red wine with 2 tablespoons lemon juice; 1 small onion, peeled and sliced; 1 bay leaf; few sprigs fresh parsley, thyme, oregano. Season with freshly ground pepper and mix with ½ cup [125 ml / 4 fl oz] oil. Pour over the poultry joints in a dish and leave to marinate for several hours or overnight in the refrigerator. One way to ensure the marinade seeps round the joints is to place the joints with the marinade in a large plastic bag. Turn every few hours allowing the mixture to flow round the joints. Retain the liquid for basting toward the end of cooking.

Petti di pollo alla valdostana

Chicken Breasts with Fontina

⌦ 00:15   00:20 ⌦

American	Ingredients	Metric/Imperial
4	Chicken breasts	4
½ cup	Milk	125 ml / 4 fl oz
	Flour	
2 tbsp	Butter	25 g / 1 oz
2 tbsp	Vegetable oil	1 ½ tbsp
	Salt and pepper	
½ cup	Dry white wine	125 ml / 4 fl oz
4	Thick slices of fontina cheese	4

1. Flatten the chicken breasts by pounding, soak them in milk for 10 minutes, drain and then flour.
2. Heat the butter and oil in a frying pan (with a lid), and when really hot, slip in the chicken and brown on both sides.
3. Season well, pour in the wine and allow to evaporate. Lay 1 slice of fontina cheese on each piece of chicken.
4. Cover the pan and continue to cook until the cheese has melted. Serve very hot.

Budellette di pollo al limone

Chicken Livers with Lemon

⌦ 00:30   00:40 ⌦

American	Ingredients	Metric/Imperial
1 lb	Chicken giblets and chicken livers	450 g / 1 lb
1	Onion	1
1	Carrot	1
1	Celery stalk	1
¼ lb	Mortadella	100 g / 4 oz
¼ cup	Butter	50 g / 2 oz
	Salt and pepper	
2 ½ cups	Chicken stock	600 ml / 1 pint
2	Egg yolks	2
1	Lemon	1
3 tbsp	Chopped parsley	2 tbsp

1. Wash the giblets well in hot water, chop finely.
2. Slice the onion, carrot and celery and cut the mortadella into thin strips; sauté in the heated butter. Add the giblets and season with salt and pepper. Cover with stock, bring to the boil then lower the heat and simmer for about 35 minutes.
3. Beat the egg yolks, add lemon juice and a little of the cooking liquid, mix well. Pour into the pan with the livers.
4. Stir well, remove from the heat and serve immediately, sprinkled with chopped parsley. Serve with rice or toast.

Petti di pollo fritti

Chicken Breasts Fried in Batter

	00:30 Marinating time 01:30	00:08

American	Ingredients	Metric/Imperial
½ tsp	Chopped bay leaves	½ tsp
½ tsp	Chopped rosemary	½ tsp
1	Garlic clove	1
⅔ cup	Olive oil	150 ml / ¼ pint
1	Lemon	1
	Salt and pepper	
4	Chicken breasts	4
½ cup	All purpose (plain) flour	50 g / 2 oz
1	Egg	1
½ cup	Milk	125 ml / 4 fl oz
	Vegetable oil for frying	
	Lemon wedges	

1. Chop bay leaves and rosemary, crush the garlic and put in a bowl with the olive oil, lemon juice, salt and pepper.
2. Immerse the chicken breasts and marinate for 1½ hours turning from time to time.
3. Prepare a fairly thick batter by whisking flour, beaten egg and milk with a pinch of salt.
4. Coat the chicken breasts with batter. Heat some vegetable oil in a deep frying pan and when it is really hot slip in the chicken breasts and cook until crisp and brown. Drain on absorbent kitchen towels.
5. Serve hot with lemon wedges and grilled tomatoes.

Petti di pollo allo sherry

Chicken Breasts in Sherry Sauce

	00:35	00:25

American	Ingredients	Metric/Imperial
4	Chicken breasts	4
	Salt	
1 tbsp	Flour	1 tbsp
3 oz	Parma ham	75 g / 3 oz
3 oz	Fontina cheese	75 g / 3 oz
1	Black truffle	1
2 tbsp	Olive oil	1½ tbsp
2 tbsp	Butter	25 g / 1 oz
1	Small onion	1
½ cup	Dry sherry	125 ml / 4 fl oz
1 cup	Stock	225 ml / 8 fl oz

1. Choose 4 plump breasts of chicken. Using a thin, sharp knife, open up each breast laterally to form a pouch. Flatten by pounding, season with salt and flour lightly.

2. Place 2 slices of ham (cut to fit), a thin slice of fontina and a sliver of truffle inside each one. Close and secure with toothpicks.

3. Heat the oil and butter in a large frying pan, chop the onion and sauté for 4 minutes. When the onion starts to color, add the chicken breasts and brown on both sides.

4. Pour in the sherry and allow to evaporate. Continue to cook, moistening the chicken from time to time with a little stock for a further 15 minutes. Make a gravy to serve with the chicken, using the juices from the pan.

Rosemary

Coscette di pollo alla boscaiola

Chicken Thighs Braised with Mushrooms

00:15   00:50

American	Ingredients	Metric/Imperial
4	Chicken thigh portions	4
¼ lb	Bacon	100 g / 4 oz
½ tsp	Chopped thyme	½ tsp
½ tsp	Chopped rosemary	½ tsp
	Salt and pepper	
2 tbsp	Vegetable oil	1 ½ tbsp
¼ cup	Butter	50 g / 2 oz
1	Onion	1
1	Carrot	1
1	Celery stalk	1
¼ cup	Dry white wine	50 ml / 2 fl oz
1 cup	Stock	225 ml / 8 fl oz
¾ lb	Mushrooms	350 g / 12 oz
14 oz	Peeled plum tomatoes	400 g / 14 oz
1 cup	Coffee (single) cream	225 ml / 8 fl oz
1 tbsp	Parsley	1 tbsp

1. Bone the chicken portions carefully, wash and dry; insert a slice of bacon into each with a pinch of thyme and rosemary and a little pepper. Secure with a toothpick.

2. Sauté gently in heated oil and butter until golden.

3. Chop the onion, carrot and celery and add these to the pan on a medium heat, cook for 6 minutes. Moisten with white wine, allow to bubble for 1 minute and then add the stock and the sliced mushrooms, stir well. After a few minutes, add the pulped tomatoes. Cook over medium heat for 30 minutes.

4. Remove the toothpicks and check the seasoning. (This part of the dish can be prepared well ahead of time.)

5. To serve, heat through very gently, adding a little extra pepper if necessary and pour the cream into the sauce a few moments before serving. Sprinkle with chopped parsley.

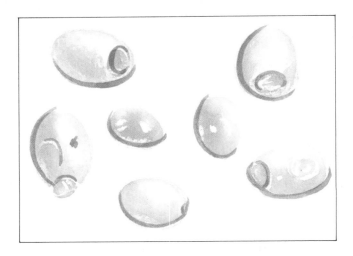

Galletti al vino

Spring Chicken in Red Wine

	00:25		01:20

American	Ingredients	Metric/Imperial
1 (3 lb)	Spring chicken	1 (1.4 kg / 3 lb)
2 oz	Bacon	50 g / 2 oz
¼ cup	Vegetable oil	50 ml / 2 fl oz
¾ lb	Button onions	350 g / 12 oz
	Salt and pepper	
	Flour	
¼ cup	Butter	50 g / 2 oz
3 tbsp	Cognac	2 tbsp
½ cup	Red wine	125 ml / 4 fl oz
2	Bay leaves	2
2	Cloves	2
1 cup	Chicken stock	225 ml / 8 fl oz
1 tbsp	Chopped parsley	1 tbsp

1. Wash and dry the chicken thoroughly and joint into small pieces.
2. Chop the bacon and sauté in a little oil; add the button onions and season with salt and pepper.
3. Flour the chicken pieces lightly. Melt most of the butter in a second pan, add the chicken and sauté until golden on all sides.
4. Transfer the onions and bacon to the pan with the chicken, stir and check seasoning. Add the cognac; flame, then add the wine, bay leaves and cloves.
5. As soon as the wine boils, add the stock, lower the heat and simmer gently for about 45 minutes.
6. When the chicken is cooked, transfer to a heated serving dish with the onions using a slotted spoon.
7. Thicken the sauce by gradually adding 2 teaspoons flour mixed with the remaining butter, beat until smooth and creamy.
8. Pour over the chicken and arrange the onions around it. Sprinkle with parsley.

Corona di pollo e olive

Chicken and Olive Ring

02:00   01:15

American	Ingredients	Metric/Imperial
1 (3¼ lb)	Small chicken	1 (1.5 kg / 3¼ lb)
Scant ¼ cup	Vegetable oil	3 tbsp
2 tbsp	Butter	25 g / 1 oz
2	Sprigs of rosemary	2
2	Eggs	2
5 oz	Piece of tongue	150 g / 5 oz
1¼ cups	Gelatin	300 ml / ½ pint
¼ lb	Green olives	100 g / 4 oz
¼ lb	Black olives	100 g / 4 oz
1	Lettuce	1
1	Bunch of watercress	1

1. Pot-roast the chicken with oil, butter and rosemary for 1¼ hours.
2. Remove from the pot, allow to cool slightly, skin and remove flesh from the bones.
3. Hard-cook (boil) eggs, cool in cold water, remove shells. Cut the tongue into strips, discarding any fat.
4. Prepare the gelatin according to the maker's instructions and put a little of it in a mold (preferably a ring mold with a hole in the middle) and refrigerate. When the gelatin in the mold has set, arrange on it the chicken, tongue, olives and the sliced or quartered eggs. Top up with the cool gelatin and refrigerate. To serve, plunge the mold quickly into water and then turn onto a serving dish lined with lettuce leaves and watercress and remove the mold.

Pollo al cartoccio

Chicken Baked in Foil

00:15   01:25

American	Ingredients	Metric/Imperial
1 (3 lb)	Chicken	1 (1.4 kg / 3 lb)
1	Garlic clove	1
1	Sprig of rosemary	1
2 or 3	Sage leaves	2 or 3
¼ cup	Olive oil	50 ml / 2 fl oz
	Salt and pepper	
3 or 4	Slices of fat tuscany ham	3 or 4
¼ cup	Sherry or brandy	50 ml / 2 fl oz

1. Preheat the oven to 350°F / 180°C / Gas Mark 4.
2. Wash and dry the chicken thoroughly. Place the garlic and herbs inside, rub all over with olive oil, sprinkle lightly with salt and pepper and cover with the slices of ham, securing with thread or fine string.
3. Place on a sheet of foil, moisten with sherry or brandy, close the foil and bake in a moderate oven for about 1¼ hours or until cooked.
4. Carve and serve hot or cold with a mixed salad.

Scaloppe di tacchino Cordon Bleu

Scallopine of Turkey Cordon Bleu

	00:20		00:25	

American	Ingredients	Metric/Imperial
4	Turkey scallopine (escalopes)	4
	Salt and pepper	
	Flour	
4	Slices of lean cooked ham	4
4	Thin slices of fontina cheese	4
½ cup	Button mushrooms	75 g / 3 oz
⅓ cup	Butter	75 g / 3 oz
3 tbsp	Olive oil	2 tbsp
1 tbsp	Chopped parsley	1 tbsp
1 cup	Chicken stock	225 ml / 8 fl oz
	Sprigs of parsley	

1. Pound the scallopine lightly to flatten, season with salt and pepper and dust with flour.
2. Cut the ham and fontina into slices the same size as the scallopine.
3. Wash and dry the mushrooms and slice thinly. Heat a little of the butter in a small pan and sauté the mushrooms lightly; set them aside.
4. Heat the remainder of the butter and all the olive oil in a pan large enough to accommodate the scallopine. Cook them for 6-7 minutes on each side.
5. Lay a slice of ham on each scallopine, scatter with mushroom slices and sprinkle with chopped parsley and a little pepper, top with slices of fontina.
6. Heat the stock and pour it over the scallopine, cover the pan and simmer for 8 to 10 minutes, by which time the cheese should have melted.
7. Serve at once, decorated with sprigs of parsley.

Tacchino al melograno

Turkey with Pomegranates

This dish is a native of the region around Venice, where pomegranate juice is available all the year round.

	00:30		02:30	

American	Ingredients	Metric/Imperial
1 (6¾ lb)	Young turkey hen	1 (3 kg / 6¾ lb)
2½ oz	Sliced bacon	65 g / 2½ oz
	Salt and pepper	
2 tbsp	Vegetable oil	1½ tbsp
¼ cup	Butter	50 g / 2 oz
3	Pomegranates	3

1. Preheat the oven to 350°F / 180°C / Gas Mark 4.
2. Choose a young hen turkey that has been well hung. Have it cleaned and wash thoroughly.
3. Lard with slices of bacon, especially over the breast. Season lightly with salt and pepper, then place in a pan with heated oil and butter. Cook for 2½ hours in the oven, basting with the strained juice of 2 pomegranates.
4. Prepare the sauce by chopping the giblets very finely, mixing with the juice of the remaining pomegranate, some oil, ½ cup [125 ml / 4 fl oz] stock, salt and pepper. Simmer over a very low heat, stirring constantly.
5. When the turkey is cooked, allow to stand for 10 minutes, then slice and serve accompanied with this delicious pomegranate sauce, strained or blended.

Cook's tip: if pomegranate juice is not available, use grapefruit. Add a few drops of red vegetable coloring to deepen the color of the sauce.

Cotolette di tacchino e speck

Turkey Rissoles

00:30
Plus chilling

00:16

American	Ingredients	Metric/Imperial
3	Thick slices of white bread	3
¼ cup	Milk	50 ml / 2 fl oz
1¼ lb	Turkey meat	600 g / 1¼ lb
3 oz	Fat bacon	75 g / 3 oz
2	Eggs	2
1 tbsp	Grated parmesan cheese	1 tbsp
1 tsp	Worcester sauce	1 tsp
½ tsp	Cayenne pepper	½ tsp
½ tsp	Mixed herbs	½ tsp
1 tbsp	Flour	1 tbsp
½ cup	Dried bread crumbs	50 g / 2 oz
⅔ cup	Frying oil	150 ml / ¼ pint
	Salt and pepper	

1. Soak the bread in the milk, squeeze out the excess moisture.
2. Grind (mince) the turkey and the bacon fat together, add 1 beaten egg, grated parmesan cheese, Worcester sauce, cayenne pepper, mixed herbs and mix well with the bread. Form into 8 rissoles using floured hands.
3. Now beat the remaining egg with 2 tablespoons [1½ tablespoons] water on a flat plate and sprinkle the bread crumbs on another plate. Dip the rissoles in the egg and then in bread crumbs and chill in the refrigerator for 30 minutes.
4. Heat the oil in a frying pan over a high heat, slip in 4 rissoles and reduce heat slightly. Fry for 4 minutes each side, drain onto absorbent kitchen towels and keep warm. Reheat the oil and fry the remaining rissoles. Season and serve with lemon wedges.

Cook's tip: A quick dish which can be made from left-over pieces of turkey, chicken or game. Mix in the food processor to save time.

Tacchino alla diavola

Devilled Turkey

00:30
Marinating time 06:00
Serves 6

01:00

American	Ingredients	Metric/Imperial
1 (3 lb)	Turkey joint	1 (1.4 kg / 3 lb)
2/3 cup	Olive oil	150 ml / 1/4 pint
2	Garlic cloves	2
1	Sprig of parsley	1
	Salt and pepper	
Scant 1/4 cup	Spicy mustard	3 tbsp
1	Onion	1
4 – 8	Large fresh mushrooms	4 – 8

1. Marinade the turkey joint in olive oil with the crushed garlic cloves, a chopped sprig of parsley and seasoning.
2. Leave for at least 6 hours, turning several times.
3. Preheat the oven to 400°F / 200°C / Gas Mark 6. Oil a baking pan and cook the turkey for 30 minutes.
4. Remove from the oven and brush with a mixture of spicy mustard and finely chopped onion. Reduce heat to 350°F / 180°C / Gas Mark 4.
5. Surround the turkey with mushrooms brushed with remaining marinade and cook for a further 30 minutes.

Tacchinella tartufata

Turkey with Truffle

00:40

03:00

American	Ingredients	Metric/Imperial
1 (6 lb)	Young hen turkey	1 (2.7 kg / 6 lb)
	Salt and pepper	
1/4 lb	Pork fat	100 g / 4 oz
1/2 cup	Ground (minced) veal	100 g / 4 oz
1/2 cup	Ground (minced) pork	100 g / 4 oz
1	Truffle	1
1/4 cup	Butter	50 g / 2 oz
Scant 1/4 cup	Olive oil	3 tbsp

1. Preheat the oven to 400°F / 200°C / Gas Mark 6.
2. Wash and dry the turkey, sprinkle salt and pepper inside.
3. Prepare a stuffing either by chopping or make in the food processor. Chop the pork fat and combine it with the ground (minced) veal and pork, the turkey liver and half the truffle, finely sliced.
4. Stuff the turkey and sew up the aperture.
5. Cut the rest of the truffle into slivers and insert these under the skin of the bird, spacing them as evenly as possible. Rub the entire surface with butter.
6. Cook in a roasting pan in the oil and butter for 3 hours, basting from time to time with the pan juices. Remove from the oven, allow to stand for 10 minutes, carve and serve hot with roast potatoes and gravy made from pan juices.

Fesa di tacchino alla valdostana

Turkey Breasts with Ham and Cheese

| | 00:30 | | 00:30 | |

American	Ingredients	Metric/Imperial
1 ¼ lb	Turkey breasts	600 g / 1 ¼ lb
1	Egg	1
½ cup	Dried bread crumbs	50 g / 2 oz
¼ cup	Butter	50 g / 2 oz
Scant ¼ cup	Oil	3 tbsp
¼ lb	Parma ham	100 g / 4 oz
¼ lb	Fontina cheese	100 g / 4 oz
	Salt and pepper	
1 tsp	Thyme	1 tsp

1. Divide the turkey breasts into 4 escalopes, flatten with a cutlet bat, add to the beaten egg and leave to soak for 30 minutes.

2. Preheat the oven to 350°F / 180°C / Gas Mark 4.

3. Coat the turkey carefully with bread crumbs, patting the crumbs in place. Sauté in the heated butter and oil on a medium heat until golden.

4. Drain on absorbent kitchen towels then lay in an oven-proof dish. Place a slice of ham and several thin slivers of cheese on each piece of turkey, sprinkle with a pinch of salt, pepper and thyme and place in the hot oven until the cheese has melted — about 20 minutes. A little grated truffle makes a tasty but optional garnish.

Mushroom (Devilled Turkey)

Anatra all'ananas e piselli

Duckling with Pineapple and Green Peas

00:30   01:00

American	Ingredients	Metric/Imperial
1 (3 lb)	Duckling	1 (1.4 kg / 3 lb)
Scant ¼ cup	Vegetable oil	3 tbsp
¼ cup	Butter	50 g / 2 oz
1	Onion	1
1	Garlic clove	1
¼ cup	Flour	25 g / 1 oz
¾ lb	Canned pineapple	350 g / 12 oz
	Salt and pepper	
3	Tomatoes	3
¼ lb	Mushrooms	100 g / 4 oz
½ lb	Peas, frozen	225 g / 8 oz

1. Wash and dry the duckling, cut into 4 portions with poultry shears.
2. Put into a pan with hot oil and brown all over. Turn the heat down and turn to cook evenly.
3. Carve the joints and remove as much of the flesh as possible from the bones.
4. Heat the butter in the same pan, sauté the chopped onion and a crushed clove of garlic for 4 minutes then add the duck meat. Sprinkle with flour and stir well.
5. Add the juice of the pineapple, mix and season well. Tip in the skinned, mashed tomatoes and the sliced mushrooms; simmer for 30 minutes.
6. Lightly cook the peas. Dice the pineapple chunks and add, with the peas, to the pan. Cook for a further 15 minutes and serve piping hot.

Anatra all'arancia

Duck with Orange Sauce

00:35   01:15

American	Ingredients	Metric/Imperial
1 (4½ lb)	Medium-sized duck	1 (2 kg / 4½ lb)
3 tbsp	Olive oil	2 tbsp
¼ cup	Butter	50 g / 2 oz
	Salt	
1 cup	Vegetable stock	225 ml / 8 fl oz
1	Lemon	1
6	Oranges	6
2	Sugar cubes	2
3 tbsp	Wine vinegar	2 tbsp

1. Preheat the oven to 400°F / 200°C / Gas Mark 6.
2. Singe, clean and wash the duck, dry very thoroughly.
3. Heat oil and butter in a casserole and brown the duck all over; add salt, pour in the stock mixed with a little lemon juice and cook in the oven for 20 minutes. Turn the heat down to

350°F / 180°C / Gas Mark 4 and cook until tender. Transfer to a plate and keep warm.

4. Squeeze 2 oranges and strain the juice. Cut the zest of the lemon into thin strips and soften by immersing in boiling water for 1 minute.

5. Sieve the cooking juices and add the orange juice and lemon zest.

6. In a small saucepan, make a caramel by melting 2 sugar cubes which have been rubbed with orange peel and adding a little vinegar.

7. Tip the sauce with the cooking juices into the caramel and heat gently, stirring, over a low heat without allowing the mixture to boil.

8. Carve the duck and arrange on a heated serving dish. Garnish with the remaining oranges, peeled, sliced and with the pips removed.

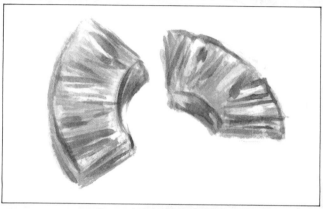

Pineapple (Duckling with Pineapple and Green Peas)

Oca arrostita alla lorenese

Roast Goose

00:25   02:00 to 02:30

American	Ingredients	Metric/Imperial
1	Small goose	1
¼ lb	Bacon	100 g / 4 oz
6	Sage leaves	6
3	Sprigs of rosemary	3
¼ cup	Butter	50 g / 2 oz
3 tbsp	Vegetable oil	2 tbsp
	Freshly ground pepper	

1. Preheat the oven to 350°F / 180°C / Gas Mark 4.

2. Scald, pluck and clean the goose. Flatten slightly by pounding. Cut half the bacon into strips and put some inside the goose and some on the breast and legs, securing with toothpicks.

3. Using the prongs of a fork to make little holes, insert sage leaves and rosemary under the skin.

4. Place the goose in a roasting pan with several knobs of butter and some oil. Roast for 2 hours, baste from time to time.

5. Test by pricking with a fork; if any liquid runs out, you will need to cook the bird a little longer.

6. Transfer to a warm serving dish, dust with freshly-ground pepper and serve with roast potatoes.

Oca con salsa di peperoni

Goose with Sweet Pepper Sauce

00:30   01:35

American	Ingredients	Metric/Imperial
1	Small goose	1
3 tbsp	Vegetable oil	2 tbsp
2 tbsp	Butter	25 g / 1 oz
6	Sage leaves	6
6	Sprigs of rosemary	6
½ cup	Dry white wine	125 ml / 4 fl oz
	Salt and pepper	
¼ lb	Salami	100 g / 4 oz
2	Large sweet peppers	2

1. Preheat the oven to 400°F / 200°C / Gas Mark 6.

2. Clean and skin the goose (this is not too difficult if you have a sharp knife and a little patience). Reserve the liver and the emptied and cleaned stomach (optional).

3. Place the goose in a roasting pan with the oil and rub with butter, sage and rosemary. Brown all over in oven and season.

4. Allowing 15 minutes cooking time per 1 lb / 450 g and 15 minutes extra continue to cook until tender. Moisten with wine from time to time.

5. Carve the goose into 8 pieces and place on a dish in a warm place. Retain the cooking juices, you will need them for the sauce.

6. Chop the salami finely, together with the bird's stomach, (optional), liver, and the peppers, deseeded. Skim off as much fat as possible from the cooking juices, strain and add the chopped ingredients; cook over a medium heat for 15 minutes.

7. Add the finely chopped goose liver and a few twists of the pepper mill. Check the seasoning and stir until all the ingredients are cooked.

8. Serve the goose accompanied by the hot sauce.

Oca con le mele renette

Roast Goose with Apples

00:15 02:15

American	Ingredients	Metric/Imperial
1	Medium-sized goose	1
2 lb	Canadian apples	1 kg / 2 lb
¼ cup	Olive oil	50 ml / 2 fl oz
1 cup	Dry white wine	225 ml / 8 fl oz
	Salt and pepper	

1. Preheat the oven to 350°F / 180°C / Gas Mark 4.
2. Singe, clean, wash and dry the goose. The skin may be removed which will considerably reduce the fat content.
3. Peel, core and dice half the apples and place them in the cavity of the goose. If you have left the skin on, sew up the aperture; if not, bind with a strip of foil.
4. Place in an oiled roasting pan and roast, baste occasionally.
5. After 1½ hours, pour wine over the goose, vaporize, season with salt and pepper and return to the oven. Continue to baste from time to time for a further 30 minutes or until cooked.
6. Peel, core and slice the remaining apples, boil in very slightly salted water, strain and sieve. Serve with the goose sliced.

Oca al vino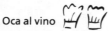

Goose Braised in Wine

00:15 02:00

American	Ingredients	Metric/Imperial
1 (3¼ lb)	Young goose	1 (1.5 kg / 3¼ lb)
	Salt and pepper	
1	Small onion	1
1	Sprig of sage	1
1	Sprig of rosemary	1
	Oil	
4	Lemons	4
2½ cups	Dry red wine	600 ml / 1¾ pints
1	Bunch of mixed herbs	1
2 tbsp	Cornstarch (cornflour)	3 tbsp

1. Preheat the oven to 350°F / 180°C / Gas Mark 6.
2. Wash the goose well, season the cavity with salt, place an onion and a sprig each of sage and rosemary inside.
3. Rub all over with oil, place in a large roasting pan, sprinkle with lemon juice and roast for about 2 hours. Turn after 30 minutes.
4. Bring the wine to the boil in a saucepan with a bunch of mixed herbs.
5. Strain and add to the goose at the end of 1 hour. Turn the bird twice during the next hour.
6. Carve the goose before serving and sprinkle with salt and pepper, but only in moderation as the goose is already highly flavored. Put the goose in the oven while you make the sauce.
7. Strain fat from cooking juices and thicken with cornstarch blended with a little water. Pour into a sauceboat and serve at once with the carved goose.

79

GAME

Faraona alla Giobatta

Guinea-Fowl in Walnut Sauce

🔪 00:30   01:00 to 01:15 🍳

American	Ingredients	Metric/Imperial
1 (2 lb)	Guinea-fowl	1 (1 kg / 2 lb)
¼ cup	Vegetable oil	50 ml / 2 fl oz
1 oz	Capers	25 g / 1 oz
2	Garlic cloves	2
¼ tsp	Chopped rosemary	¼ tsp
¼ tsp	Chopped sage	¼ tsp
¼ tsp	Chopped basil	¼ tsp
1 cup	Dry red wine	225 ml / 8 fl oz
	Salt and pepper	
1 cup	Stock	225 ml / 8 fl oz
¼ cup	Butter	50 g / 2 oz
1 tbsp	Cognac	1 tbsp
¼ cup	Flour	25 g / 1 oz
½ cup	Walnuts, shelled and chopped	50 g / 2 oz
½ cup	Milk (optional)	125 ml / 4 fl oz

1. Wash and dry the guinea-fowl, put into a large saucepan with oil and brown quickly over a fairly high heat.
2. Chop the capers, garlic, rosemary, sage and basil and sprinkle over the bird, then add the wine and season with salt and pepper.
3. Lower the heat, add stock and simmer until tender.
4. Prepare the sauce by melting the butter in small pan, then, away from the heat, add the cognac, flour, chopped walnuts and a pinch of salt. Return the pan to the heat and cook this mixture for a few minutes adding stock from the bird and the milk. Mix well and heat through for a further 2 minutes.
5. Arrange the guinea-fowl on a heated serving dish, carve and pour the walnut sauce over the bird.

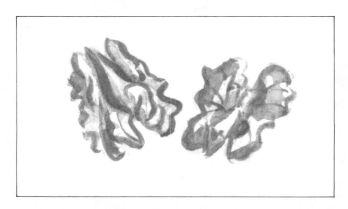

Faraona alla panna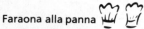

Guinea-Fowl in Fresh Cream Sauce

	00:25		01:30
American	**Ingredients**	**Metric/Imperial**	
1 (3¼ lb)	Guinea-fowl	1 (1.5 kg / 3¼ lb)	
¼ lb	Bacon or parma ham with fat	100 g / 4 oz	
½ cup	Butter	100 g / 4 oz	
1	Celery stalk	1	
2	Small carrots	2	
1	Onion	1	
¼ tsp	Chopped rosemary	¼ tsp	
¼ tsp	Chopped thyme	¼ tsp	
¼ tsp	Chopped marjoram	¼ tsp	
2	Bay leaves	2	
	Salt and pepper		
½ cup	Dry white wine	125 ml / 4 fl oz	
1 cup	Stock	225 ml / 8 fl oz	
1 cup	Coffee (single) cream	225 ml / 8 fl oz	

1. Wash and dry the guinea-fowl and wrap the bacon or ham around it.
2. Melt the butter in a large, heavy pan, add the fowl and brown on all sides.
3. Chop the vegetables finely and add them, with the herbs to the pan. Season with salt and pepper. After a few minutes, add the wine and let it bubble, then add a little stock, lower the heat, cover and simmer for about 1¼ hours.
4. When the bird is cooked, transfer to a board, carve and then arrange on a heated serving dish.
5. Pour the cream into the pan, allow the sauce to thicken but not boil; sieve or blend, reheat and pour over the guinea-fowl.

Faraona alla panna e al marsala

Guinea-Fowl with Cream

	00:10		01:20
American	**Ingredients**	**Metric/Imperial**	
1 (3 lb)	Guinea-fowl hen	1 (1.4 kg / 3 lb)	
¼ cup	Butter	50 g / 2 oz	
½ cup	Marsala wine	125 ml / 4 fl oz	
	Salt and pepper		
1¼ cups	Coffee (single) cream	300 ml / ½ pint	

1. Singe the bird, wash and dry both inside and outside.
2. Melt the butter in a heavy pan, add the fowl and brown all over, moistening with the marsala, a little at a time. Allow the marsala to vaporize; season with salt and pepper and cook on a low heat for 50 minutes, adding the cream very gradually.
3. Remove the guinea fowl and keep warm. Reduce the liquid in the pan slightly. Cut the bird into 4 pieces, arrange on a heated serving dish and top with the fragrant sauce.

Starne arrosto

Roast Partridge

🔪 00:20   01:00 to 01:25 🍲

American	Ingredients	Metric/Imperial
2	Partridges	2
	Salt and pepper	
¼ lb	Chicken livers	100 g / 4 oz
1	Slice of ham	1
2 tbsp	Butter	25 g / 1 oz
1 tbsp	Cognac	1 tbsp
¼ tsp	Chopped thyme	¼ tsp
2	Thin slices of fat bacon	2
2	Vine leaves	2
	Fried bread	

1. Wipe the partridges and season the cavity.
2. Prepare the stuffing for the partridges by washing and chopping the chicken livers with those of the partridges.
3. Chop the ham, mix with the butter, chicken livers, the cognac, a pinch of thyme, salt and pepper. Put half of this mixture in each partridge and sew it up.
4. Wrap the birds in a thin slice of fat bacon and a vine leaf, then truss the partridges and cook on the spit or in a very hot oven (475°F / 240°C / Gas Mark 9.) When the partridges are almost cooked, remove the binding and bacon and brown over a brisk heat.
5. Cut in half and serve on slices of crisp fried bread.

Composta di piccioni

Pigeon Compote

🔪 00:25   01:15 🍲

American	Ingredients	Metric/Imperial
4	Pigeons	4
7 oz	Pork fat	200 g / 7 oz
	Butter	
2 tbsp	White flour	15 g / ½ oz
1 cup	Stock	225 ml / 8 fl oz
2	Bay leaves	2
2	Sprigs of thyme	2
5	Sprigs of parsley	5
	Salt and pepper	
16	Small onions	16
¼ lb	Dried mushrooms	100 g / 4 oz
1⅓ cup	Green olives, stoned	225 g / 8 oz

1. Wash the prepared pigeons. Heat the diced pork fat and butter, brown the pigeons.
2. Stir in the flour, allow it to color slightly then add the stock, bay leaves and sprigs of thyme and parsley; season with salt and pepper.
3. Add the onions, stir, cover and simmer on a low heat for about 40 minutes.

4. Wash the dried mushrooms and soak for at least 15 minutes in warm water. Add to the pigeons with the green olives, simmer for a further 20 minutes and remove herbs.

5. Serve the pigeons with boiled rice or pasta accompanied by a salad made from several different kinds of lettuce.

Piccioni alle cipolle

Pigeons in Onion Sauce

00:30   01:30

American	Ingredients	Metric/Imperial
4	Young pigeons	4
Scant ¼ cup	Vegetable oil	3 tbsp
¼ cup	Butter	50 g / 2 oz
1 ¼ lb	Onions	600 g / 1 ¼ lb
	Salt and pepper	
1	Sprig of thyme	1
1	Bay leaf	1
14 oz	Canned tomatoes	400 g / 14 oz

1. Wash the pigeons, cut each one into half, lengthwise. Heat the oil and butter in a large pan and brown the halved pigeons on either side.

2. Lower the heat and continue to cook slowly for 15 minutes. Remove from the pan and keep warm.

3. Chop the onions and put them into the same pan with a little more oil and allow to color slightly. Return the pigeons to the pan, season well with salt and pepper and crumble in the thyme and bay leaf, add tomatoes and break down with a spoon. Cover and cook over moderate heat for about 30 minutes, stirring from time to time.

4. As soon as the pigeons are done, arrange on a heated serving dish with the sauce poured over the top. A little water or stock may be added to clear the pan juices for the sauce.

Cook's tip: This dish requires less attention if cooked in the oven for 40 minutes until pigeons are tender at 325°F / 170°C / Gas Mark 3 from stage 3.

Vine leaf (Roast Partridge)

Redcurrants

Pernici in salmì alla padovana 👨‍🍳 👨‍🍳

Salmis of Partridges Paduan-Style

	01:00		01:40
	Hanging time 8 days		

American	Ingredients	Metric/Imperial
4	Partridges	4
½ cup	Butter	100 g / 4 oz
3	Carrots	3
1	Sprig of rosemary	1
8	Slices of fat bacon	8
⅔ cup	Olive oil	150 ml / ¼ pint
1	Head of celery	1
1	Onion	1
2	Bay leaves	2
	Livers (from the partridges)	
¼ cup	Marsala wine	50 ml / 2 fl oz
¼ lb	Mushrooms	100 g / 4 oz
	Salt and pepper	
3 tbsp	Red currant jelly	2 tbsp

1. Draw the partridges, keeping the livers and hang for 8 days in a dark place.

2. Pluck, singe, wash and lightly salt the inside of the bird.

3. Stuff with a mixture of a little butter, finely chopped carrots, rosemary and cover with 2 slices of bacon.

4. Heat half the butter and oil and brown the birds.

5. Heat the remaining butter and oil and cook the rest of the chopped carrot, celery and the onion with 2 bay leaves. Then add the chopped livers and, after a few minutes, sprinkle with marsala, cover and cook for 15 minutes. Rub through a sieve or blend.

6. Preheat the oven to 400°F / 200°C / Gas Mark 6.

7. Arrange the partridges on an oiled baking pan or large casserole. Pour over the vegetables and liver, put in a hot oven for 15 minutes. Reduce the temperature to 350°F / 180°C / Gas Mark 4. Cover and cook for 1 hour.

8. Remove birds on to a heated serving dish and keep warm.

9. Add 1¼ cup [300 ml / ½ pint] water or stock to the dish and scrape all the juices, reduce to make a gravy.

10. Slice the mushrooms very thinly. Pour the sauce into a pan and heat with the mushrooms for 3 minutes, season, then add red currant jelly. Serve the birds hot with the sauce.

Fagiano arrosto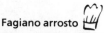

Roast Pheasant

American	Ingredients	Metric/Imperial
1	Pheasant	1
¼ lb	Fat bacon	100 g / 4 oz
½ cup	Butter	100 g / 4 oz
1 cup	Milk	225 ml / 8 fl oz
3	Slices of white bread	3
3	Cloves	3
	Salt	
1	Onion	1

1. Pluck and singe the pheasant. Lard the breast and legs with the bacon, and put on the spit, moistening continually with melted butter.
2. Serve the pheasant accompanied simply by its cooking juices or by the following bread sauce.
3. Boil the milk and add the bread, the onion studded with cloves, salt, 1 tablespoon [15 g / ½ oz] of butter and cook for 15 minutes. Stir well, remove the onion and mix well.
4. Carve the pheasant and serve with the bread sauce, roast potatoes and steamed broccoli.

Fagiano alla romana

Roman-Style Pheasant

American	Ingredients	Metric/Imperial
7 oz	Sweetbreads	200 g / 7 oz
1	Onion	1
7 oz	Chopped veal	200 g / 7 oz
¼ cup	Melted butter	50 g / 2 oz
½ tsp	Chopped sage	½ tsp
½ tsp	Chopped rosemary	½ tsp
1 tbsp	Grated parmesan cheese	1 tbsp
1	Egg, beaten	1
2	Pheasants	2
5 oz	Fat bacon	150 g / 5 oz
½ cup	Vegetable oil	125 ml / 4 fl oz
1 lb	Boiled potatoes	450 g / 1 lb

1. Preheat the oven to 350°F/180°C/Gas Mark 4.
2. Chop sweetbreads and onion and combine with the veal, butter, sage, rosemary, parmesan and bind together with beaten egg. Stuff cavity of pheasants with forcemeat.
3. Cover pheasant breasts with fat bacon, place in a roasting pan, brush with oil and cook for about 1½ hours, basting with oil from time to time.
4. Pierce flesh of birds to check juices are clear, then remove stuffing in one piece. Slice thickly. Joint pheasants into 4. Place pheasant joints on a hot serving dish, surround with stuffing and boiled potatoes and pour over cooking juices.

Fagiano alla piemontese

Pheasant Piedmont-Style

	00:25		01:30

American	Ingredients	Metric/Imperial
1 (2 lb)	Pheasant	1 (1 kg / 2 lb)
⅓ cup	Butter	75 g / 3 oz
1	Sprig of rosemary	1
	Salt and pepper	
6	Slices of bacon	6
¼ cup	Marsala wine	50 ml / 2 fl oz
7 oz	Black olives	200 g / 7 oz

1. Preheat the oven to 350°F / 180°C / Gas Mark 4.
2. Clean the pheasant, wash carefully and dry.
3. Mix half the butter with the rosemary and season, place inside the pheasant. Wrap the bird in the slices of bacon and truss it. Put in an ovenproof dish with the remaining butter, cut into pieces. Cook until golden brown in the oven, basting occasionally with marsala wine and the cooking juices.
4. Remove the stones from the olives, take the bird from the oven, add the olives and cook for a further 30 minutes over a moderate heat on the stove.
5. Remove the pheasant, untie and carve on a board. Cut the bacon into pieces. Arrange the bird and bacon on a heated serving dish, add the olives and serve.

Fagiano alla cacciatora

Hunter's Pheasant

	00:20		02:00

American	Ingredients	Metric/Imperial
¼ lb	Fat bacon	100 g / 4 oz
1	Carrot	1
2	Celery stalks	2
¼ lb	Raw ham	100 g / 4 oz
1	Onion	1
2 oz	Dried mushrooms	50 g / 2 oz
Scant ¼ cup	Vegetable oil	3 tbsp
1 tbsp	Butter	1 tbsp
2	Oven-ready well hung pheasants	2
½ cup	Brandy	125 ml / 4 fl oz
	Stock if needed	

1. Chop bacon, carrot, celery and ham finely, and slice onion. Soften dried mushrooms in tepid water, then drain.
2. Heat oil and butter in a large pan and sauté onion for 2 minutes. Add pheasants to pan and brown all over. Pour over brandy and add bacon, carrot, celery and ham to pan, with mushrooms.
3. Cover and cook over a low heat for about 2 hours, adding stock to the pan to prevent the ingredients drying out.

4. Transfer pheasants to a hot serving dish using a slotted spoon. Place vegetables around birds, pour juices over pheasants serve accompanied by puréed green vegetables tossed in butter.

Beccacce alla re Enzo

King Enzo's Woodcocks

This is an ancient recipe dating back to King Enzo's imprisonment in Emilia.

⬭▭▭ 00:25   01:15 ⬭

American	Ingredients	Metric/Imperial
2	Onions	2
4	Garlic cloves	4
	The giblets	
½ cup	Lard	100 g / 4 oz
1 tsp	Chopped sage	1 tsp
1 tsp	Chopped rosemary	1 tsp
4	Dressed woodcocks	4
1 tbsp	Vegetable oil	1 tbsp
½ cup	Grappa	125 ml / 4 fl oz
1 cup	Whipping (double) cream	225 ml / 8 fl oz
¼ tsp	Pepper	¼ tsp
¼ tsp	Cinnamon	¼ tsp
¼ tsp	Unsweetened cocoa	¼ tsp
1 lb	Cooked potatoes for purée	450 g / 1 lb
1 cup	Milk	225 ml / 8 fl oz
½ cup	Butter	100 g / 4 oz
	Salt	
¼ tsp	Nutmeg	¼ tsp
1	Lemon	1

1. Chop the onions and 2 cloves of garlic finely, chop giblets and beat into the lard with sage and rosemary. Insert into cavity of woodcocks and using fine string and a trussing needle sew up birds to prevent filling escaping.
2. Heat oil and cook remaining garlic for 1 minute, then remove. Add woodcocks to pan and brown all over. Pour over grappa and lower heat. Cover and leave to cook over a low heat for 40 minutes.
3. Preheat oven to 450°F / 230°C / Gas Mark 8. Beat cream, pepper, cinnamon and cocoa together. Transfer woodcocks to a deep fireproof dish, pour over cream sauce, cover and cook a further 10 minutes over a low heat.
4. Prepare a purée of potatoes by mashing cooked potatoes with milk, butter, salt, nutmeg, grated lemon. Spoon into a forcing bag fitted with a ½ in / 1 cm star vegetable nozzle and pipe a border of potato around dish.
5. Place dish in the oven for 10 minutes to brown potatoe, then serve immediately.

Schidionata di quaglie

Quails on the Spit

00:35   00:15

American	Ingredients	Metric/Imperial
8	Quails	8
1 tsp	Chopped basil	1 tsp
1 tsp	Chopped rosemary	1 tsp
1	Onion	1
¼ cup	Butter	50 g / 2 oz
	Salt and pepper	
8	Slices of bacon	8
¼ cup	Vegetable oil	50 ml / 2 fl oz
	Rice	

1. Clean, singe and wash the quails. Dry and stuff with chopped basil, rosemary and onion mixed with butter.

2. Lightly season the quails with salt and pepper, then lard them by wrapping in thin slices of bacon secured with thread.

3. Put them on the spit and paint with vegetable oil. Brown the quails over a high heat, brush with the fat that falls into the dripping pan.

4. Remove from the spit at the end of the cooking time and serve with boiled rice, seasoning with the dripping pan juices.

Cook's tip: The same recipe can be used for cooking small pigeons and other small birds.

Quaglie alla pavese

Quails Pavia-Style

00:30   01:00

American	Ingredients	Metric/Imperial
12	Quails	12
	Salt and pepper	
8	Slices of bacon	8
½ cup	Vegetable oil	125 ml / 4 fl oz
4	Garlic cloves	4
½ cup	Red wine	125 ml / 4 fl oz
1⅔ cups	Rice	350 g / 12 oz
1½ quarts	Chicken stock	1.5 litres / 2½ pints
2 oz	Ox marrow	50 g / 2 oz

1. Clean and singe the quails, season and cover them with slices of bacon.

2. Heat the oil, cook the birds with the crushed garlic until golden, sprinkle with the red wine as they turn brown.

3. Remove the quails after 25 minutes cooking and put them to one side.

4. Brown the rice in the pan juices from the quails, stirring frequently. As soon as the rice has browned, sprinkle with boiling stock and add the ox marrow. Continue cooking the rice so that it is 'al dente', then arrange it on the bottom of an ovenproof dish. Lay the quails on top of the rice, put in the oven or under the broiler (grill) for 5 minutes and serve immediately.

Fantasia di pollo e quaglie

Chicken and Quail Surprise

🔪 00:25　　　　　　00:45 🍲

American	Ingredients	Metric/Imperial
4	Quails	4
4	Chicken breasts	4
¼ cup	Butter	50 g / 2 oz
¼ cup	Vegetable oil	50 ml / 2 fl oz
2 oz	Bacon	50 g / 2 oz
½ tsp	Chopped rosemary	½ tsp
2 cups	Mushrooms	200 g / 7 oz
2 cups	Béchamel sauce	450 ml / ¾ pint

1. Cut the quails in half and cook with the chicken breasts, in a large pan with the heated butter and oil. Turn from time to time until golden on each side and cooked through. Add the chopped bacon and rosemary.
2. Wash the mushrooms, slice thinly and sauté in a small pan with a little butter for 5-6 minutes.
3. Prepare a béchamel sauce, add the mushrooms.
4. Arrange the chicken and quails on a serving dish, top with mushroom sauce and serve very hot surrounded by a garnish of triangles of toast.

Quaglie alla cacciatora

Huntsman's Quails

🔪 00:30　　　　　　00:45 🍲

American	Ingredients	Metric/Imperial
8	Large quails	8
½ cup	Butter	100 g / 4 oz
1 tsp	Chopped sage	1 tsp
8	Cloves	8
½ tsp	Nutmeg	½ tsp
4	Garlic cloves	4
8	Slices of bacon	8
¼ cup	Brandy	50 ml / 2 fl oz
8	Slices of polenta	8

1. Clean the quails, singe and remove their intestines.
2. Mix half the butter with the chopped sage, cloves, nutmeg and chopped garlic, divide into 4.
3. Place a portion inside each bird. Wrap the quails in the slices of bacon and secure with toothpicks.
4. Sauté them in a frying pan with butter, browning them evenly. Sprinkle with brandy, cover the pan and continue cooking for 15 minutes.
5. When the cooking is completed, put a lighted match to the pan and allow the excess alcohol to burn off completely.
6. Serve the quails immediately on slices of hot polenta on a heated serving dish.

Leprotto alla siciliana
Sicilian Hare

| | 00:30 | 01:00 to 01:30 | |

American	Ingredients	Metric/Imperial
1	Young hare	1
¼ lb	Grated ewe's milk cheese	100 g / 4 oz
⅔ cup	Sultanas	100 g / 4 oz
7 oz	Black olives	200 g / 7 oz
½ cup	Vegetable oil	125 ml / 4 fl oz
	Bilberry sauce (optional)	
Sauce		
1 lb	Bilberries	225 g / 8 oz
1 tsp	Mustard	1 tsp
1	Egg yolk	1

1. Preheat the oven to 400°F / 200°C / Gas Mark 6.
2. Thoroughly clean a young hare.
3. Chop up the usable intestines, add ewe's milk cheese and washed sultanas. Stir the pitted (stoned) black olives into the mixture and fill the belly of the hare. Cooking can take place in a hot oven for 1 hour or on the spit for 1½ hours, whichever is preferred, basting with the oil.
4. The hare is served sprinkled with the very hot pan juices and accompanied by a sweet spicy bilberry sauce. Rub bilberries through a strainer with mustard and egg yolk and serve in a sauceboat.

Coniglio in porchetta Valsavaranche
Stuffed Rabbit Valsavaranche

| | 00:45 | 01:30 | |

American	Ingredients	Metric/Imperial
1	Small rabbit	1
1½ cups	Ground (minced) meat (can be left-overs)	350 g / 12 oz
¼ tsp	Chopped rosemary	¼ tsp
¼ tsp	Chopped sage	¼ tsp
2 tbsp	Grated parmesan cheese	1½ tbsp
2	Eggs	2
	Salt and pepper	
2	Garlic cloves	2
1	Onion	1
⅓ cup	Vegetable oil	4 tbsp
1 cup	Cream	225 ml / 8 fl oz
Scant ¼ cup	Vinegar	3 tbsp

1. Open the rabbit lengthwise, making a cut under the belly so that you can clean it thoroughly.
2. Grind (mince) the edible rabbit offal together with the meat and a little rosemary and sage. Add the grated parmesan and eggs to obtain a soft stuffing mixture and season.

3. Fill the rabbit with the stuffing, sew up the opening well.
4. Preheat the oven to 325°F / 170°C / Gas Mark 3.
5. Crush the garlic and chop the onions and fry in heated oil for 5 minutes, push to one side.
6. Raise the heat, put in the rabbit and brown on all sides. Moisten a little at a time with the cream mixed with the vinegar to form a thick sauce, which should not stick. (If necessary dilute with a little stock or hot water.) Cover and cook the rabbit for 1 hour in the oven.
7. Place the rabbit on a heated serving dish. Strain the sauce through a sieve and serve in a sauceboat.

Bilberries (Sicilian Hare)

Coniglio selvatico alla sarda

Sardinian Wild Rabbit

00:20   01:20

American	Ingredients	Metric/Imperial
1 (1½ lb)	Small rabbit, jointed	1 (700 g / 1½ lb)
1	Onion	1
Scant ¼ cup	Vegetable oil	3 tbsp
	Salt and pepper	
½ cup	Water	125 ml / 4 fl oz
2 cups	Dry white wine	450 ml / ¾ pint

1. Joint rabbit and remove liver and chop. Peel and chop onion. Heat oil in a fireproof dish and sauté onion for 2-3 minutes to brown rabbit joint. Season with salt and pepper and cook over a low heat, adding water. Cover and cook for about 1 hour over a low heat.
2. Add liver to pan and white wine, cover and continue cooking for about 10 minutes.
3. Serve the rabbit on a hot serving dish, pour juices over.

Arrosto misto di selvaggina

Mixed Roast Game

	00:20	00:20

American	Ingredients	Metric/Imperial
2 lb	Mixed game : venison, hare, wild rabbit, young wild boar	1 kg / 2 lb
	Seasoned flour	
¼ cup	Vegetable oil	50 ml / 2 fl oz
¼ cup	Cognac	50 ml / 2 fl oz
	Salt and pepper	
¼ tsp	Paprika	¼ tsp
2	Lemons	2
	Chopped parsley	

1. Preheat the oven to 425°F / 220°C / Gas Mark 7.
2. Cut game into equal sized pieces, toss in seasoned flour, thread onto a spit or large skewers. Brush with oil and place threaded skewers on a baking sheet.
3. Place in oven for 15-20 minutes, sprinkle with cognac from time to time, and turn occasionally.
4. Whisk pepper, salt and paprika into lemon juice. Put cooked skewers on a large hot ovenproof plate and pour lemon sauce over. Garnish with chopped parsley and serve.

Cervo alla Vatel

Venison Vatel-Style

	00:20 Marinating time 08:00	04:00

American	Ingredients	Metric/Imperial
4 quarts	Red wine	4 litres / 7 pints
1	Large bunch of mixed herbs	1
	Salt and pepper	
2 tsp	Powdered cinnamon	2 tsp
1	Onion	1
4½ lb	Venison	2 kg / 4½ lb
½ cup	Coffee (single) cream	125 ml / 4 fl oz
¼ cup	Cognac	50 ml / 2 fl oz

1. Pour red wine into a large bowl, add herbs, salt, pepper, cinnamon and sliced onion. Add venison to bowl and leave overnight to marinate.
2. Transfer venison and marinade to a fireproof casserole dish. Bring to boil, cover and simmer over a low heat for about 2 hours until liquid has reduced by a half. Remove meat and put on one side. Strain or purée sauce in a blender.
3. Return meat and sauce to casserole dish, cover and cook a further 2 hours over a low heat. Just before serving, season with salt and pepper, stir in cream and cognac and serve immediately.

Capriolo in umido alla pastora

Shepherd's Venison Stew

This typical game dish originates from the Val d'Aosta region, and makes a delicious autumn meal.

🔪 **00:25**
Standing time 12:00

03:00 🍲

American	Ingredients	Metric/Imperial
2 lb	Pieces of venison	1 kg / 2 lb
	Seasoned flour	
⅔ cup	Vegetable oil	150 ml / ¼ pint
	Salt and pepper	
¼ tsp	Chopped thyme	¼ tsp
2	Bay leaves	2
¼ tsp	Chopped rosemary	¼ tsp
¼ tsp	Chopped sage	¼ tsp
1 quart	Red wine	1 litre / 1¾ pints
4	Carrots	4
4	Onions	4
4	Celery stalks	4
2	Potatoes	2
2	Leeks	2
1	Shallot	1
14 oz	Small button onions	400 g / 14 oz

1. Cut venison into bite-size pieces, toss in seasoned flour. Heat oil in a fireproof casserole dish and, when very hot, brown meat all over with salt, pepper, thyme, bay leaves, rosemary and sage.

2. Pour over red wine, cover and simmer for 2 hours. Allow to cool and refrigerate overnight.

3. Peel and chop carrots, onions, celery, potatoes, leeks and shallot. Add these to venison and allow to simmer for 30 minutes, stirring from time to time. Meanwhile clean small onions and add to pan and cook a further 30 minutes.

4. Strain meat from sauce and put on one side. Purée sauce in a blender or food processor, return to casserole dish, replace meat and reheat for 5 minutes.

5. Serve hot with polenta, rice, boiled or puréed potatoes.

INDEX